LESSONS FROM THE GOLDEN AGE OF
CLASSROOM FILMSTRIPS

CHANGE YOUR UNDERWEAR TWICE A WEEK

DANNY GREGORY

ARTISAN
NEW YORK

Every reasonable attempt has been made to contact owners of copyright. Errors of omission will be corrected in subsequent editions.

Published by Artisan
A Division of Workman
Publishing, Inc.
708 Broadway
New York, New York 10003
www.artisanbooks.com

Library of Congress Cataloging-in-Publication Data

Gregory, Danny, 1960–
    Change your underwear twice a week : lessons from the golden age of classroom filmstrips / by Danny Gregory.
        p. cm.
    ISBN: 1-57965-263-8
    1. Filmstrips in education. 2. Education—Effect of technological innovations on. I. Title.

    LB1043.8.G74 2004
    371.33'52—dc22

                        2003063916

Acknowledgments:

PJ Mark, Patti Lynn Gregory, Paul Sahre, William van Roden, Rick Prelinger of Prelinger Archives, and all the folks at Artisan

Printed in China

10 9 8 7 6 5 4 3 2 1

Book design by:

William van Roden
and Nicholas Caruso

This book was set in:

Akzidenz Grotesk, Minion, and Vinyl

For Pipsi and Miranda

FOCUS

HOMEROOM

HEALTH AND HYGIENE

SOCIAL STUDIES

MATH AND SCIENCE

IN WHICH we learn that math and science aren't just for eggheads, and that getting a man on the Moon was the only thing protecting Earth from becoming a completely Red planet.

Making Change

Why Things Float

Electricity at Home

The Earth: A Great Storehouse

Earth's Blanket of Air

The Earth and Its Movements

Why Does It Rain, Snow, Hail, and Sleet?

The Meaning of Fractions

Expanded Notation

Our Neighbor, the Moon

How Man Explores Space

Earth's Satellite, the Moon

The Moon—Our Nearest Neighbor in Space

Work of Astronomers and Space Travel

Life on Other Planets

PROPAGANDA

IN WHICH we see how Corporate America snuck into the classroom in a teacher suit.

Your Daily Bread

Tommy Takes a Train Trip

Railroads and National Defense

Railroads and Clothing

Railroads and Our Mail

Railroads and the Food We Eat

How We Get Our Cotton

How We Get Our Rubber

How to Ride Your Bicycle Safely

WHAT EVER HAPPENED TO FILMSTRIPS?

IN WHICH there may or may not be a final pop quiz.

A DAY ON THE FARM

FOCUS

Maybe you remember this ritual.

First, a projector would be sitting by the teacher's desk, perhaps in a big case, pebbled maroon or hospital green or slate gray with brushed aluminum trim and several hasps more than a normal valise—a mute clue that today would be different.

Then the teacher would make an announcement. "All right, class,

A filmstrip about a filmstrip.
From *School Workers: The Pupil*,
page 37

we're going to look at a filmstrip now, all about milk and where it comes from. Let's get set up." She'd reach up over the blackboard behind her desk, next to where the pull-down map of the forty-eight states was coiled, and unfurl the projector screen.

She'd signal to one kid, then hand him a long pole with a blunt brass hook on one end. He'd fish around near the ceiling until he snagged the cord that rolled down the shades. The room would become dimmer as each successive window was covered.

Soon the room would be reduced to shadows and silhouettes, and your classmates, empowered by their invisibility, would murmur to each other and shift in their wooden seats. You knew you could relax; it was unlikely you'd be called upon to perform. You'd be learning communally in the dark, focused as a group, passively taking it all in. Yeah, right.

Meanwhile, the teacher would have left her customary place at the front of the room to carry the heavy case up the center aisle. She would stop near the middle of the room, put the projector on someone's desk, then lower its little front feet. "You're going to be my helper today," she would say to the desk's hapless resident and hand him the end of the projector's power cord. He would snake the cable past giggling, whispering classmates, crouching and feeling for the wall socket in the dark.

Next the filmstrip would emerge from its colored plastic case, a little gossamer spool of 35-mm film, like a strip of negatives from a camera. The teacher would feed the end of the strip into the projector, probably with some difficulty, past a maze of sprockets and gears. She then would flip some toggle switches, a fan would whir, and a diffused beam would splash onto the screen. Bright white light would also leak out of the sides of the projector, illuminating the teacher and the student whose desk she had commandeered.

As she twiddled the lens, the image would get clearer, then soften again, until finally the ➜

blur became a picture. Sometimes it would be upside down and backward, prompting moans from everyone. Finally, a graphic of crosshairs and the word *FOCUS* would materialize, sharp on the screen.

The filmstrip would scroll forward, past several frames that said simply "Start," then the title would appear: "The Story of Milk." Sometimes the narrative would come from a warped audiotape or a scratched record, vaguely amplified by the projector's tinny speaker. The track would pause periodically and beep, a signal to the projectionist to advance to the next frame. Often, this sequence would get screwed up, and the story and images would be hopelessly out of sync.

Most filmstrips were silent. The teacher would read aloud each subtitle and discuss the content of each frame, firing questions into the darkened room, forcing the class to shake off its torpor. Sometimes she would wander into the stream of light, her face and dress splattered with parts of a cow or a diagram of a cell, while her silhouette stalked across the screen, a black giant lurking in a dairy or a post office or a corner of the solar system.

The filmstrip began as a magic lantern—an oil lamp and a glass slide containing one or more frames that could project a painted image onto a wall to illustrate a story. In time, the glass gave way to celluloid, and the images became photos. Businesses used them to train workers and managers—they were the PowerPoint of their day.

During World War II, filmstrips went mainstream. A single strip could be produced and reproduced to uniformly teach millions of GIs the proper way to use a rifle or avoid contracting syphilis. Back home, their wives and sisters were being turned into factory workers by the same simple medium, which was teaching them the proper way to use a rivet gun or avoid contracting syphilis.

Girls having fun breathing.
From *Earth's Blanket of Air,*
page 151

Though this same technology had been in schools for decades, it wasn't until after the war that educational filmstrips became the rage. Well, not really a rage. The medium was far too humble to excite anyone all that much. Teachers, however, preferred it to other technologies because it was lightweight, simple to set up, and flexible enough to incorporate into a lesson plan. Principals liked it because it was cheap and hardy.

But as with most technologies introduced to the classroom, it is generally the "experts" rather than the educators who are excited by them. In the last century, radio, film, television, and computers all held out enormous promises—most of them yet to be fulfilled. Thomas Edison, for example, believed that the real revolutionary effect of film would be in education, not entertainment. Films, he claimed, were far more efficient ways to teach, covering every possible subject and driving home lessons in ways that would stir the emotions. "Books will soon be obsolete in the public schools. It is possible to teach every branch of human knowledge with the motion picture," he said in 1913.

In the last two centuries, many more experts have cropped up: academic entrepreneurs who emerge from their ivory towers to market new systems and approaches, foundations hoping to increase their relevance, reformers wishing to replace teachers with machines to lower the cost of education or fight off some newly perceived threat—the Soviet Union, labor unions, Japan, juvenile delinquency.

Businesses have held out promises, too. They've made great claims for their films, tapes, and software and saddled schools with expensive equipment, projectors, televisions, speakers, and computers, not to mention the service contracts to keep them going.

Who decides which of these "miracles" will be used in the classroom? It's rarely the long-suffering teachers, who have little time to learn how to operate, repair, and maintain all this gear, ➔

Based on these laws, the path of a moon missile is calculated today.

The moon—it's right there!
From *The Moon—Our Nearest Neighbor in Space*, page 177

and aren't convinced of its merit in the first place. They are, however, the first to get the blame when all of this valuable innovation gathers dust in a closet. The fact is, the more complex and intrusive the technology, the less apt it is to help the process of educating children.

Despite Edison's prediction, educational motion pictures never caught on in a big way and certainly couldn't replace textbooks. Most teachers simply didn't like them: They often didn't feel comfortable with the noisy projectors and fragile film; the equipment was too expensive to have in every classroom, so it had to be shared and was often unavailable or poorly maintained. Most teachers didn't like handing over the lesson and control of the class to some machine while they stood in the dark and the kids fidgeted. Even today, few teachers rely heavily on leading-edge technology and use computers only to supplement their lesson plans.

The filmstrip was a far more benign and flexible technology than most. The projectors weren't motorized, so they were cheaper and less prone to break down and mangle the film. Teachers could get a pupil to run the projector while they stood in front of the class doing a voice-over of the lesson, customizing it to their own agendas rather than that of the films' producers. It was also a child-friendly technology; harried, bored, or substitute teachers could let students sit in small groups or by themselves and run a filmstrip viewer while the teachers busied themselves elsewhere.

Thus, the simple, durable filmstrip reigned for decades.

When I mention educational filmstrips to most people, they usually don't know what I'm referring to. But if I describe the "ding" on the tape, the little viewers we used in the library, the plastic boxes, the strips curled up inside, they invariably recall the experience in vivid detail.

Childhood returns to us through sense memories, links between the significant and insignificant data that were stuffed away all those years ago. The smell of burning toast or a

snippet of music can transport us back dozens of years to when we first encountered those
sensations. For example, the soft staticky warble of a shortwave radio being tuned reminds
me sharply of my grandmother. The taste of an overcooked hot dog with ketchup transports me
to the cafeteria in my elementary school. Sometimes the connections are impossible to unravel:
Why does the fragrance of sandalwood soap put me in a spot near my grandfather's garage? Why
do scraps of newspaper take me back to the zoo? These aren't just reminders, they're like a time
machine that sends me plunging into a flood of memories and feelings I'd forgotten.

Nostalgia isn't powerful because it projects an image of a better time and place. Rather,
it helps us see who we are today and how we came to be that way. All of those sense memories
are the tips of icebergs that are buried deep within us. Journeys to the past let us dive below the
surface to show us more simply constructed versions of ourselves. Like archaeologists scraping
down through the strata of our lives, we see ourselves when our lives were full of promise, when
our ideals were less tarnished, our eyes brighter and clearer.

Throughout life, the lessons we're taught aren't absolute, regardless of the authority
with which they're delivered. They're all guided by current wisdom, trends, perceptions, and
biases, by culture and politics, local and national policies. Even something as pure and abstract
as mathematics is taught from certain perspectives, with a certain set of goals in mind. In the
end, what we really learn in school is how to be Americans and citizens of the modern world.

The world has changed a great deal in the fifty years since many of the strips in this book
were produced—perhaps the most important fifty years in human civilization. America and the
world have undergone enormous changes since World War II, and the filmstrips we were shown
in school are brimming with clues to how those changes made us who we are. ➜

This book is designed to let you have several parallel experiences. First, you'll reencounter the filmstrips you or your parents saw in school, most of which haven't been seen since. They'll seem funny, quaint, and familiar. They have none of the sophistication of today's media and are so distilled and self-contained that they've become icons of "a simpler time" (which wasn't actually simpler at all).

Second, you'll learn about some of the people who made these films and why. Some are unusual characters. Some are solid professionals and craftsmen. All of them made many beautiful and compelling images in these strips.

Third, you'll learn the context for each lesson. Why were we being taught these things at this time? What was going on outside the classroom and how did it affect what went on inside? We'll look at our childhoods from an adult perspective and discover that many of the "facts" we've always taken for granted are in fact the product of somebody's agenda. ■

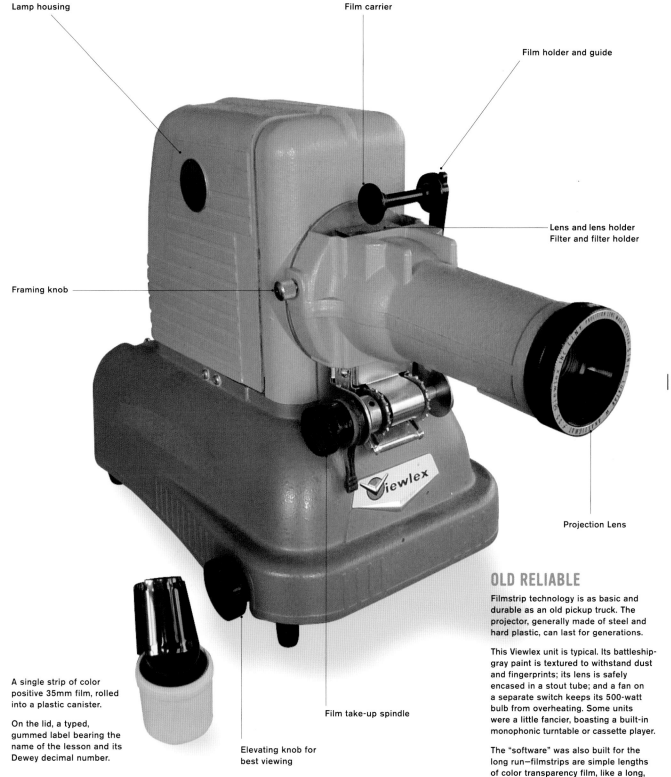

Lamp housing

Film carrier

Film holder and guide

Lens and lens holder
Filter and filter holder

Framing knob

Projection Lens

Film take-up spindle

Elevating knob for
best viewing

A single strip of color
positive 35mm film, rolled
into a plastic canister.

On the lid, a typed,
gummed label bearing the
name of the lesson and its
Dewey decimal number.

OLD RELIABLE

Filmstrip technology is as basic and
durable as an old pickup truck. The
projector, generally made of steel and
hard plastic, can last for generations.

This Viewlex unit is typical. Its battleship-
gray paint is textured to withstand dust
and fingerprints; its lens is safely
encased in a stout tube; and a fan on
a separate switch keeps its 500-watt
bulb from overheating. Some units
were a little fancier, boasting a built-in
monophonic turntable or cassette player.

The "software" was also built for the
long run—filmstrips are simple lengths
of color transparency film, like a long,
unmounted slide. Despite tears,
scratches, and dust, the show goes on.

HOMEROOM

HOMEROOM

Let's start with the basics. Why do we go to school? Or at least, why are our government and community interested in having us in school for thirteen years, and what do they expect us to be doing there?

For a long time, school was a place to learn the core curriculum: reading, 'riting, and 'rithmetic. Kids sat in rows, the teacher had a pointer (and sometimes a cane), and they would drill and drill until the students had learned the fundamentals by rote.

In the late 1890s, John Dewey established the progressive education movement. School, he said, needs to be more grounded in reality. Education isn't just about the future, but as well about the present day-to-day life of the student. It should be based on a child's needs, his or her psychological and physical development, and the real world outside the classroom. Children are not all the same, all the time, and education should take that into account.

In a progressive school, each child's development—physical, mental, social, and spiritual—is studied scientifically. The classroom is a kind of laboratory, and its findings are to be added to the body of knowledge about child development and culture. Instead of passively taking notes on teachers' lectures, students are encouraged to learn through doing, and the classroom becomes a place of experiences instead of books. The teacher, rather than being the one with all the answers, enables the students to find the answers for themselves.

Dewey also pointed out that the classroom isn't a room, it's a community, and that social activities are the context in which students will learn best. Children aren't innately concerned with great books, or great men, or the movement of the planets. They're far more interested in each other. Teachers can leverage that interest to help pupils learn for themselves and to work as a group, sharing ideas and perspectives, while the teacher coordinates and encourages.

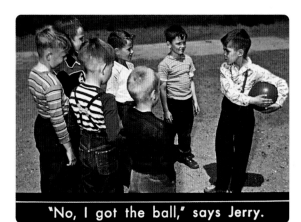

"No, I got the ball," says Jerry.

This is a democracy, Jerry. Share the ball.
From *Living and Working Together*, page 41

Now, imagine that this harmonious, curious, supportive microcosm of a community could be extended into adult society. We would learn to respect the individual and acknowledge our diversity. We would also learn to work together more productively, in spite and because of those differences, to build well-functioning communities full of active citizens all geared toward the common good.

In short, schools exist to build a better nation, the America of tomorrow, and isn't that a lot more important than memorizing the multiplication tables?

Progressivism meshed well with many other movements in the United States of the first third of the twentieth century. Corporate power and private wealth were clutched in a small number of fists, and people were increasingly suspicious of the disparities of class and wealth that were divvying up the country. FDR and the New Deal were showing that the government could be the architect of a progressive, democratic society.

Filmstrips were good tools for a progressive classroom. They were visual and experiential and could be used in an open-ended way to encourage interpretation and discussion. The very first filmstrips a pupil encountered would ease him into the experience of school at a time when he was green and anxious. As he plunged from his mother's kitchen into a room full of strangers, the filmstrip would be a reassuring guide. It would give him a condensed tour through this new world, dispel the mystery, set expectations, and lay down rules. ■

When everybody was ready, we had our milk.

24

DRINK YOUR MILK, NAP ON YOUR MAT

We Go to School

Key Productions/
Young America Films, 1952

This strip evokes what I remember best about kindergarten—the little things. Drinking from miniature bottles of milk with foil caps.❶ Rolling out my mat and napping on the classroom floor.❷ Double-sided easels with brimming cups of poster paint.❸ The smell (and taste) of thick library paste. All those books arranged on the windowsills,❹ waiting to be devoured. And tying my own shoes for the very first time.

We Go to School is a tour of a typical day in school, designed to let new pupils see what they are up against and allay their anxieties. Despite the newness of the situation, the little narrator seems quite self-assured—telling time, dressing himself, walking home unescorted, and gravely shaking hands with the adults he encounters. ➜

EXPERIENCES IN LIVING SERIES

WE GO TO SCHOOL

COPYRIGHT MCMLII BY KEY PRODUCTIONS, INC.

Today was going to be my first day at school. I wondered what it would be like.

I was up and all dressed by 7:30.

At breakfast I said I wasn't sure I wanted to go to school. But my Mother told me I would see many of my friends there.

Mother said she was coming with me and that I could take one of my toys along.

Miss Keyes said she was happy to have me in her class.

I said I would paste a cowboy picture in my clothing locker.

I watched all the things the other children were doing. Some were painting.

Some of the girls were playing with dolls.

When everybody was ready, we had our milk.

This could well have been the first filmstrip that most students saw, and it was designed to be a heartening experience. As we sat in the semidarkness, listening to the reassuring voice of the teacher, we had the chance to learn our first lesson: It was all going to be okay.

Or we could fail our first day, panicking because the lights were turned off, freaking out at the projected images (in the early 1950s many people didn't have TVs at home, and the projector could have been incredibly novel and startling), and crying hopelessly for Mommy. ∎

After a while, I told Mother I was having a good time at school, and that she could go home, now.

16

Billy showed me how easy it is to lace shoes. Then I tried it on the 'practice' shoe. 13

Miss Keyes told me I could take a tissue whenever I needed one. 14

4

After our rest period, Jerry chose a story for Miss Keyes to read. 26

It was fun to listen to the story. 27

Before we went home, we talked about what we would do tomorrow. 31

I could hardly wait to tell Mother about all the exciting things we had done in school today. 34

2

Then we rested on our mats. 25

The children clear away their toys, wash their brushes, have a stiff drink (of milk), and collapse on the floor.

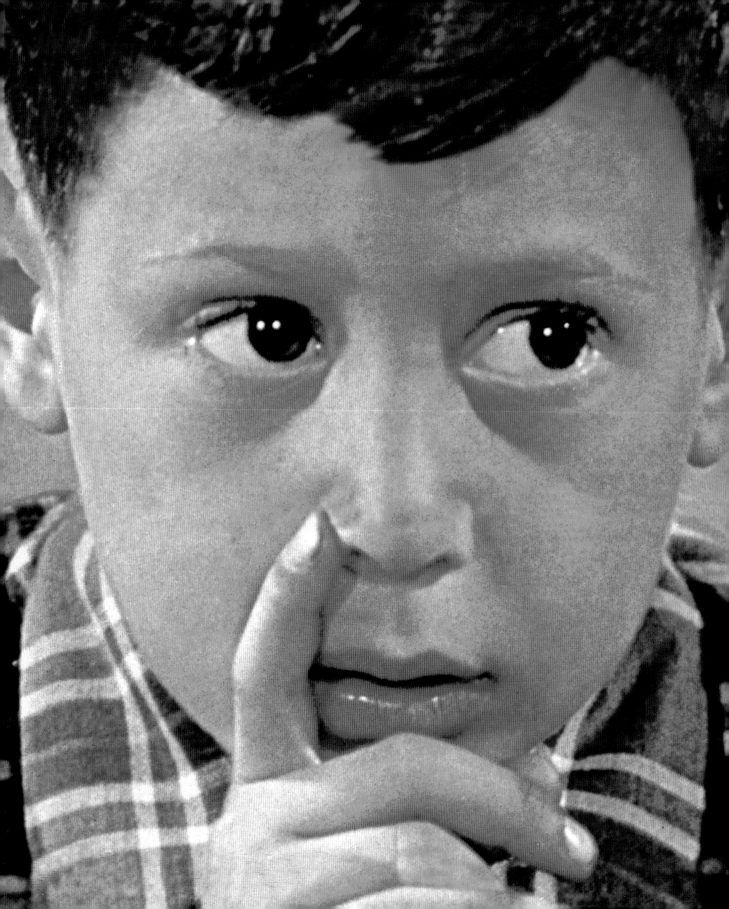

"HE'S DIFFERENT. I DON'T LIKE HIM."

The New Pupil

William P. Gottlied Co./
Encyclopaedia Britannica Films, 1952

Bosley,[1] a recent immigrant from exotic Scotland, arrives in a new school where everyone is nice and white and the teachers have monosyllabic Protestant names like Mrs. Lane,[2] Mr. Scott, and Mr. Grace. Cluelessly foreign, Bosley is befriended by a classmate named Steve,[3] who shows him around his new school and tells him to use the fire exits[4] and not make a mess of the washroom.[5] Other children are suspicious of the foreigner, who always wears a necktie, until he saves the class plants by watering them;[6] apparently his years on the farm in the high, high mountains of Scotland taught him this trick. He is now welcomed by the others, overcomes his shyness, and is very happy. →

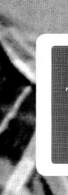

THE SCHOOL COMMUNITY

THE NEW PUPIL

In collaboration with
RUTH ELLSWORTH, Ph.D.
Wayne University

"He comes from another country. This is his first American school."

"Bosley will be our new friend," says Mrs. Lane. "I hope he'll like our class."

Then he hears a friendly voice say, "Hello, I'm Steve. I'll show you around."

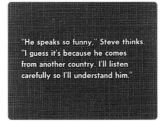

"He speaks so funny," Steve thinks. "I guess it's because he comes from another country. I'll listen carefully so I'll understand him."

Steve shows Bosley some work the boys and girls are doing.

"He's different," Lil agrees. "I don't like him."

Back inside they meet the custodian. "This is my new friend," says Steve. "I hope you'll like our school," says Mr. Grace.

Bosley feels everything is very strange.

Little by little Bosley begins to feel at home. He tells Steve about the farm he lived on.

Bosley tells Steve he took care of the flowers on his farm and that he can ride like a real cowboy. The boys become friends.

"Oh dear," says Mrs. Lane. "Our plants are almost dead. What can we do?"

"I hope so, too," says Bosley. "But everything is so strange!"

Steve sees how sad Bosley is. He wants to make him feel at home, so he shows Bosley the school.

Poor Bosley!

"This is the exit nearest our room. We use it in fire drills."

"This is the boys' washroom. You must try to keep it neat."

Steve thinks of Bosley. "Bosley can help," he says. "He knows all about plants." "I'll try," says Bosley.

Bosley soaks the plants in water. Then he puts them in a sunny spot. He waters them regularly.

He does a good job. "See how pretty they are now," says Mrs. Lane.

"We're lucky to have you in our class, Bosley."

This lesson was preparing Steve and his classmates for a tsunami of such clueless foreigners. Starting in 1950, immigration to the United States began to rise dramatically, with a quarter of a million newcomers arriving on our shores each year, the largest influx since the 1920s. The Immigration and Nationality Act of 1952, however, established new quotas on who got in from where. The argument for keeping out people from Eastern Europe and Asia was "to preserve the sociological and cultural balance of the United States." Right. Refugees, though, were given dispensation, and more than two hundred thousand escapees from war-torn Europe and the descending iron curtain arrived over the next few years. Most were Italians, Germans, Yugoslavs, and Greeks. Bosley was one of very few refugees from Scotland; most Scots came after the Cromwellian Civil War of 1641.

This filmstrip, produced by Encyclopaedia Britannica Films, was created just after World War II by William Benton, who began his career in advertising. He founded the famous Benton & Bowles agency, which introduced the radio soap opera, and retired a rich man at age thirty-six. Then he became a vice president of the University of Chicago, the seat of progressive and visual education (John Dewey had taught there). When Sears, Roebuck decided to sell its interest in Britannica, the entrepreneurial Benton put up the money, then acquired the educational film archives of Kodak and an educational filmmaker, ERPI, from Western Electric.

Before long, EBF was a giant. From its studio in Wilmette, a Chicago suburb, it produced several thousand films and filmstrips for the educational markets from 1944 to 1990. It relied on freelancers to write and produce the films, including folksinger Joan Baez's father and Elmore Leonard, master of hard-boiled suspense. ■

A CHILD'S WORK IS NEVER DONE

School Workers: The Pupil

University Films/ McGraw-Hill Films, 1969

For some reason, this filmstrip sets out to convince schoolkids that they can't just slack off, eat paste, and occasionally make circus animals out of construction paper. Instead, they're workers, employed at their own schooling. They may not be paid, but they're expected to produce. Their boss, the teacher, is blessed with an extremely small class of ethnically diverse and self-sufficient pupils.

Beyond book learning and pumpkin sketching,❶ these little workers are also expected to take responsibility for their environment—scrubbing pots and pans,❷ stacking boxes,❸ and making little shivs in the machine shop.❹ All these lessons are meant to prepare them for jobs of the future working as dishwashers, stevedores, and butchers.

School Workers is typical of filmstrips from the late 1960s—it's closer to progressive ideals than those of the preceding decade. It was designed to invite open interpretation and discussion ➜

The job of pupils is to learn.

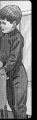

The kids learn to hang up their coats, straighten the classroom, and paint in perfect sync.

of each scene, encouraging children to reach their own conclusions, rather than providing many subtitles that lecture them on the correct way to behave. (Compare it with the next strip, *Living and Working Together.*) It's also far more multicultural than the snow-white world of earlier strips.

Though many filmstrips were assembled exclusively by the photographers and illustrators who provided the content, some of them used bona fide academic advisers to lend them guidance and credibility. Dr. Clyde F. Kohn, the chairman of the University of Iowa's geography department, supervised *School Workers'* edifying globe-handling scene.**❺**

(There's a nice self-referential moment when the teacher uses a filmstrip projector in the filmstrip.**❻**) ∎

READ MORE BOOKS

There are many other workers in the school. It looks like this boy is drawing a knife on one of them.

Tom and Nancy eat lunch at school.

STAY IN LINE, KEEP TO THE RIGHT

Living and Working Together

The Jam Handy Organization, 1954

This lesson emphasizes the value of collaboration and cooperation and the lonely misery of selfishness. The children learn to patiently wait in line to recycle [1] and treat Enn,[2] a foreign kid, as if he were really one of them. Jerry hogs a rubber ball [3] and drives his friends away. When he is willing to share, of course, he has far more fun. After the kids wait in several more lines, [4] [5] [6] they return to class. The world is orderly and harmonious, even for foreigners like Enn, and selfish Jerry quickly learns the value of getting in line.

The filmstrip is a little stiff and remote, typical of the Jam Handy Organization. Henry Jamison "Jam" Handy was a pioneer in the industry at the beginning of the century, when the spread of electricity and motion picture technology transformed visual communication. After ➜

There is fresh, cold milk in the lunchroom.

"Come and eat with us, Enn," says Nancy.

Enn has come from far away to live in our country.

After lunch, the children file out to
the playground.

Eat more slowly, Tom.

"May we play?" asks Tom.

Papers go here. Bottles go there.

Here comes Jerry with the big ball.

The girls like to play hopscotch.

Look at Miss Price.

Tom gets in line behind Nancy.

Do you know how to drink
from a fountain?

"No, I got the ball," says Jerry.

Jerry finds that it is more fun to share the ball.

One step at a time. Look ahead.

Keep to the right.

In the room the children talk until it is time to work.

he was booted out of University of Michigan, he went to work for his father, an editor of the *Chicago Tribune.* There he saw the great struggle between labor and big business firsthand and made it his mission to mend this rift using modern communications tools.

Handy left the newspaper business to learn from other pioneers, including John Bray, who patented filmstrips and developed them into a way to standardize training, and John H. Patterson, the founder of National Cash Register, who collected tens of thousands of glass lantern slides and assembled them into sequences to train his workers to be more efficient. He produced cartoons to educate audiences on the benefits of modern appliances and helped to develop training materials for U.S. troops in World War I.

In 1917, Handy started his own business, which continued to make films and filmstrips until the 1970s, most famously the classic *Rudolph the Red-Nosed Reindeer.* He set up his headquarters in Detroit to service the auto manufacturers, churning out training and sales films, brochures, and manuals. His crew of five hundred did work for the big industrial corporations RCA and DuPont, pioneered stop-motion animation (using poseable puppets) and hand-drawn cel animation for TV commercials, and created loads of short films and strips for schools. During World War II alone, they produced seven thousand training films for the armed services.

Handy, a maverick and an eccentric, lived to be ninety-seven. He is the only person to have won Olympic medals twenty years apart: a bronze at the age of eighteen in the crawl at the 1904 St. Louis games, and another in water polo in the 1924 Paris games, where teammate Johnny Weissmuller also won medals. Later in life, he decided that pockets were a waste of space and fabric, so he had all of his suits made without them. Unfortunately, he doesn't seem to have produced any filmstrips on the subject. ∎

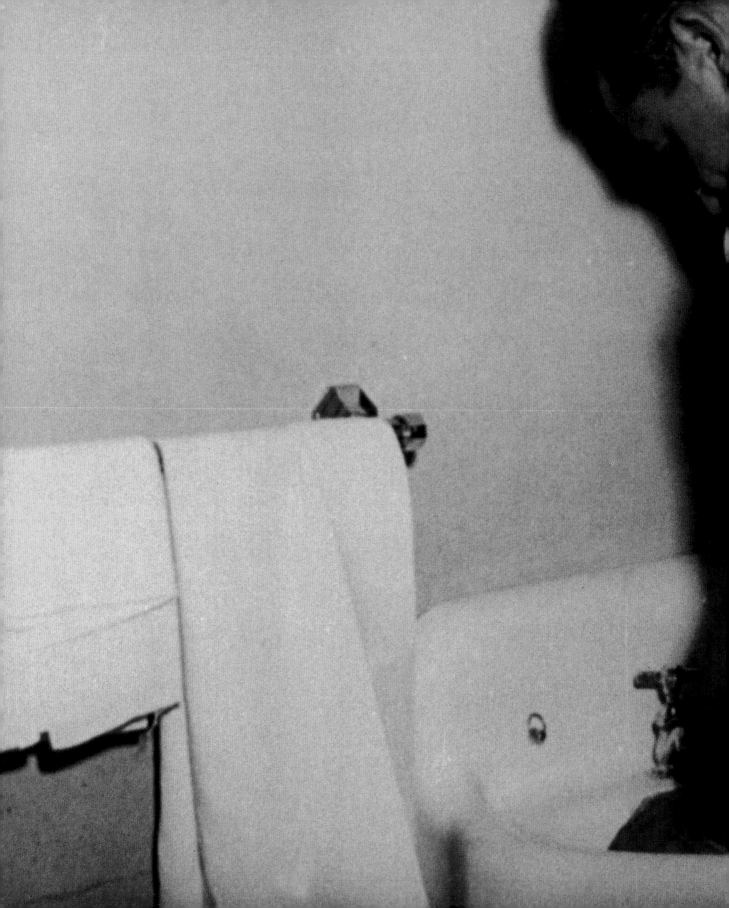

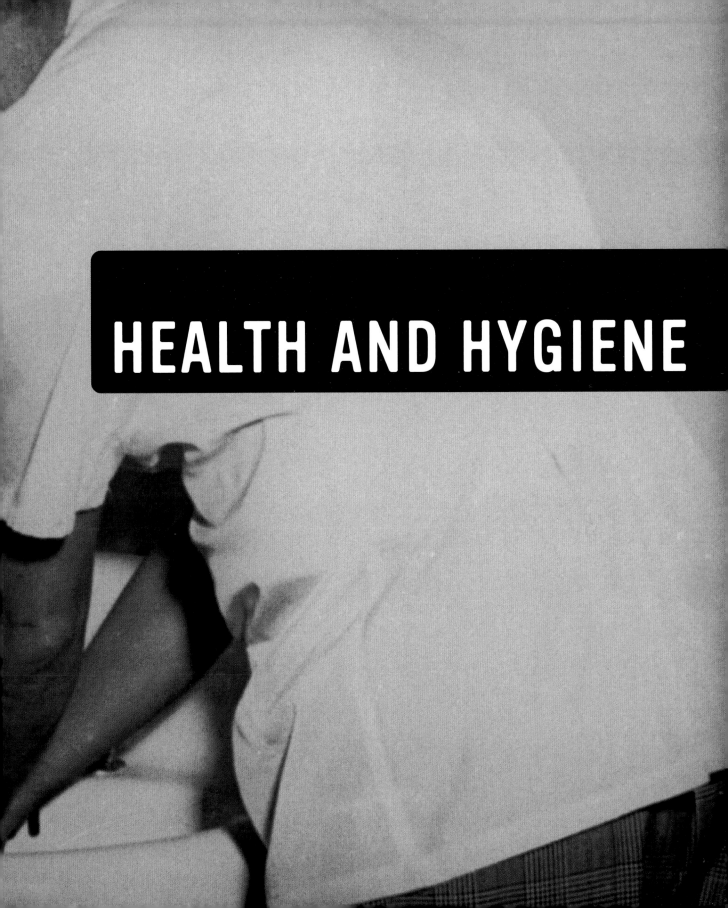

HEALTH AND HYGIENE

HEALTH AND HYGIENE

Before the progressive revolution, people assumed that the function of school was to teach a child things he or she didn't learn at home: reading and writing, some math and science, a little geography and history. Cleaning your ears, wearing a sweater, eating your veggies seemed to be the rightful domain of your mom and dad, not your teacher. Progressivism encouraged schools to form more of a bridge to the home and to pay more attention to the entire scope of the child's development, including extracurricular activities and social and physical development.

Further, that development could be interpreted in different ways—not only of the child's own best interests but also those of his or her society, or even of those who run it. And once that door was opened, new agendas were introduced. After all, if the classroom was no longer just about book learning, and schools rather than parents were molding the citizens of tomorrow, well, there was no end to the tinkering that could be done.

During the Great Depression, as the economy unraveled and farms went belly up, there weren't enough jobs to go around for all the adults who needed work. And the last thing the government wanted was an influx of cheap teenage labor competing with workers of voting age. So youngsters were strongly encouraged to stay in school, where they were creating jobs (for educators, cafeteria workers, custodians, and school board members) rather than taking them. The problem was, this couldn't be a state-subsidized baby-sitting service. What would children do in school for more and more years? To fill their days, the "Life Adjustment" curriculum was born.

Schoolchildren would be taught useful things: how to dress, how to fit in with each other, how to stay healthy, how to be workers. They'd learn about all aspects of their society, about different roles and responsibilities, about how each was essential. They'd be taught to be industrious, to spend money wisely, to stand up straight. They'd be the proving ground for new ideas on nutrition, health care, and social organization. It all seemed pretty progressive, right?

Not really. "Life Adjustment" curricula assumed that the large majority of pupils lacked

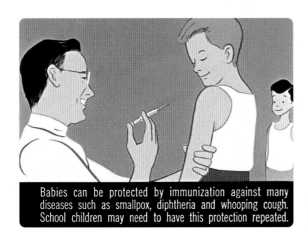

Babies can be protected by immunization against many diseases such as smallpox, diphtheria and whooping cough. School children may need to have this protection repeated.

There are few things as fun as lining up for shots at school.
From *Keeping Well and Happy,* page 49

the resources, the brains, or the motivation to go to college or to enter any sort of skilled profession and the work they'd end up doing was bound to be repetitive and mindless.

Of course, this assumption was unspoken, and nobody wanted the mass of students to feel stigmatized. The program was probably fine for the smarter, upwardly mobile minority as well. After all, only a few would become doctors and lawyers; better to prepare students for reality by giving them basic coping skills—how to wear their galoshes and drink their milk.

The deeply anti-intellectual mood of the times translated into suspicion of abstraction and anything not patently "useful," so traditional subjects—history, literature, foreign languages, and the arts—were played down. Whenever academic topics such as language and science were taught, pains were taken to make them seem practical and everyday.

This radical approach had a highly conservative goal: to mold children to fit into existing slots, under the guise of self-actualization. For much of the 1940s and 1950s, this was the main thrust of public education in America, instilling the same bland values in all of us.

There was also little attention paid to the shockingly inferior educational standards of the schools that taught African Americans, whose underfunded and inferior schools were adjusting their lives and expectations for a role at the bottom of American society. There was no need to dangle higher standards in front of them; a decent education might just cause them undue pain, as they would never be able to achieve the potential it would create for them.

Instead of achieving Dewey's goals and encouraging the diversity that has always been a cornerstone of America, education in the 1950s was dedicated to socialization and conformity. More dangerously, it wasn't addressing the growing service sector or the need for skilled, educated technology workers. Soon, most Americans would no longer be employed in mindless assembly-line work, and schools would slip increasingly out of touch with reality. ∎

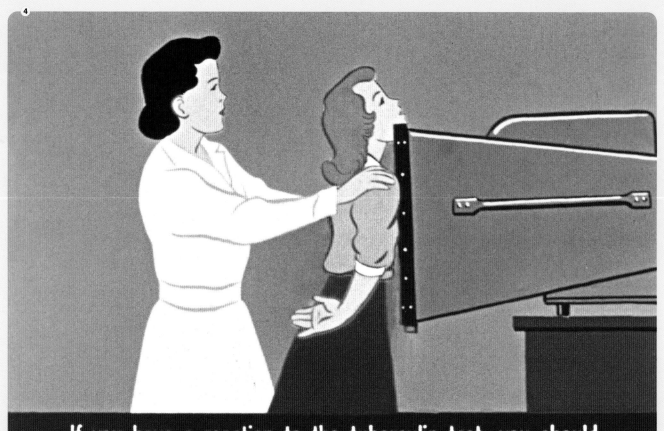

If you have a reaction to the tuberculin test, you should then have a chest X-ray to find out if the germs have begun to do harm.

DON'T PUT PENCILS UP YOUR NOSE

Keeping Well and Happy

Training Films, 1950s

This is a filmstrip from "your local Tuberculosis Association," crammed with advice on better living: Make sure you're ravenous,[1] cheerful, and growing. Get lots of fresh air and sunshine.[2] Eat a massive breakfast. Be neat and you'll be happy.

The drawings are cheery, but their content is somewhat sinister. We see smiling boys getting injections from a smiling doctor.[3] Then a nurse shoves a girl into some sort of tabletop X-ray machine.[4] The tone of the strip is far from child-friendly; it bombards the viewer with warnings about everything from time management to book care, all in the name of germ control.

Still, at a time when people were learning to be afraid of polio, atom bombs, and Reds, kids were quite used to no-nonsense warnings on how to behave. People had known that tuberculosis was contagious for five hundred years, but short of a little bloodletting ➜

Sleep ten to eleven hours a night.
Keep the room temperature between
sixty-eight and seventy-two.

hungry
d if you

In order to keep well, one of the things you should do is to play out of doors every day. Outdoor play is fun, and it helps keep your body in good working order.

2

Another thing you should do is get plenty of sunlight. Sunlight makes you feel fit and it can help prevent many diseases. But beware of getting too much.

Wash your hands often, always before eating and always after going to the toilet. Get that fresh, clean look that comes from regular use of soap.

Here are the seven kinds of food you should use to build the day's meals. Eat some food from each group every day.

Germs can pass from one person to another on things you touch; so try to keep hands and pencils away from your mouth and nose.

If you do get sick, obey the doctor's orders. If he says to go to bed and let your body rest, do so and try to forget about work and play.

1

HOT LUNCH

VEGETABLE SOUP
A GREEN VEGETABLE
BREAD AND BUTTER
SCRAMBLED EGGS
POTATOES
MILK

BOX LUNCH

SANDWICHES OF EGG
OR CHEESE OR MEAT

AN APPLE OR OTHER RAW
FRUIT OR VEGETABLE

MILK AND COOKIES

Eat a good lunch at home or at school. Don't hurry while you are eating. Play quiet games afterward.

Breakfast: eggs, cereal, toast, milk, an orange. Lunch: soup, more eggs, bread, potatoes, a vegetable.

MEAT OR FISH, POTATOES, VEGETABLE, SALAD, BREAD AND BUTTER, MILK, PUDDING.

Eat a good dinner. It's fun to help your mother plan meals, using the basic seven foods every day.

Plan your time so you will be able to do all the things you want to do and ought to do. Have a regular time for play and study, for homework and household chores.

Have a health examination once a year or whenever your doctor thinks best. Then if there is anything wrong and it is discovered early, you will have a better chance to get well quickly.

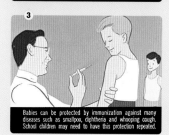

Babies can be protected by immunization against many diseases such as smallpox, diphtheria and whooping cough. School children may need to have this protection repeated.

You can find out if certain germs already have entered your body. For example, the tuberculin test is an easy way to find out if tuberculosis germs are inside your body.

You can help others to keep well and happy by being neat and clean, by being careful not to spread germs, and by doing your part cheerfully.

Help to make your home a pleasant place by helping your mother with the dishwashing and the dusting, and by taking good care of your clothes and books.

and some leeches, not much was done to treat this awful disease. In the late nineteenth century, the microorganism that caused TB was discovered, though it wasn't until about the time of this filmstrip that antibiotics were first shown to be fairly effective. Despite this emerging treatment, it was still a good idea to encourage kids to keep other people's pencils out of their noses and to "get that fresh, clean look that comes from regular use of soap."

The strip is based on a booklet, *Ways to Keep Well and Happy,* one of many penned by Dr. Ruth M. Strang of Columbia University. Her other titles include *Growing Up Healthily, Keeping Healthy, Let's Be Healthy, Living Healthfully, Wise Health Choices, Health Secrets, Health Knowledge, Health Problems, Health Through Science, Healthful Ways, Habits Healthful and Safe, Adventures in Health,* and *Health in a Power Age.*

Guess what? They were all about health. ■

51

Why must I go to sleep so early?

29

WHY ARE THEY TELLING US WHAT TO EAT?

How to Grow Well and Strong

Popular Science Publishing Company, Inc., 1953

The suggestions made in this strip seem fairly odd today. Urging kids to roast in the sun (long before sunblock and SPFs),[1] to fuel up on bread and fat,[2] and to keep their windows open at night[3] seems a pretty bizarre way to be spending our tax dollars. As for John's experiment to deprive hamsters of sleep,[4] well, that's downright barbaric.

The government started telling us what to eat in the early 1920s. The Bureau of Home Economics (part of the Department of Agriculture until World War II) set out to explain to Americans that proper nutrition depended on what, as well as how much, they consumed. It devised a set of diet plans for various socioeconomic levels, all centering on twelve different food groups. ➔

HOW TO GROW WELL and STRONG

What a large lunch! Do you think we have all the good things to eat? Let's look.

Whole wheat bread again, Mary. Wh[y] does mother give us so much bread?

Just as gas makes a car go, bread gives us heat and energy to work and play.

Fat also gives us energy. That's why, I have butter, cream and peanuts. 10

These fruits will give us vitamins to make us grow. 13

Now I know why you are so strong, John. You always eat cheese, eggs, fish and meat. 15

Why must we drink so much milk? 16

. Why
d? 6

Do you know that sunlight helps children to grow? It is as necessary as food for growth.

How would you like to try an experiment with sleep? We can start tomorrow morning.

In a short time they were all in the pet shop. Mother chose two hamsters.

We will use a bell to disturb the sleep of the hamster in the first cage.

There is no bell near this cage. This hamster will get plenty of sleep.

In 1941, the Recommended Dietary Allowances (RDA) were introduced, and the basic twelve shrank to the basic seven. The new guidelines were promoted in pamphlets published by the Department of Agriculture and taught in all schools. Meat, poultry, fish, eggs, dried beans, and peanuts were now just one group; butter and margarine were another; milk was a third; and there were four different groups of vegetables.

The basic four arrived in 1956. Fruit and vegetables had declined from almost half of the original twelve basic groups to just one of the four. Lobbyists from the meat and dairy industries had created a healthier diet for themselves, but probably not for the rest of us. ∎

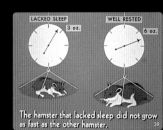
The hamster that lacked sleep did not grow as fast as the other hamster.

STINKY BOY MAKEOVER

Cleanliness and Health
Clearvue, Inc., 1975

A multiracial team of meddling clean freaks[1] takes a dirty, smelly, friendless boy[2] on an educational tour[3] of his own filthy skin and scares him into cleaning up his act.

This strip uses cartoon hyperbole rather than the dour and haranguing nurses of earlier ones on the topic. Still, the story is nearly hallucinogenic as the kids tramp around the boy's epidermis,[4] slogging through swamps and soap storms[5] in their groovy white suits[6] and gas masks. The Saturday morning cartoon style is typically 1970s and multiculturally politically correct. ■

1. Run your hands up and down your back

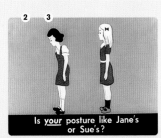
2 3. Is *your* posture like Jane's or Sue's?

4. We need 12 hours sleep each night.

6. Sue eats sweets just before meals.

Sometimes, we rest at school.

7. So, she is not hungry at supper time.

8. Good food would help her bones and muscles to be strong.

5. Look at Jim—he stays up *too* late.

9. Swinging helps them.

STAND UP STRAIGHT

Straight and Tall

Transfilms/Young America
Films, 1946

Just a year after we won World War II, a new enemy threatened America's future: bad posture. The battle plan: Make sure young people relax more. This bewildering lesson begins with Bob, stripped to the waist and caressing his spine. [1] He and his pal Jane [2] are paragons of virtue, while Jim and Sue [3] are bound for lives of deformed misery.

We see healthy kids slumped over their desks napping, then enjoying a mandatory twelve hours a night of shut-eye. [4] In a later frame, [5] Jim is chastised for staying up late. Is he boozing? Playing dice? Raising heck? No, he's quietly reading a book in an overstuffed armchair. The next morning, this wastrel sits groggily on his bed, no doubt ruing his night of easy pleasure.

Sue's vice is eating sweets. We see her tucking into a slice of cake at 5:00 P.M., [6] then refusing her dinner. [7] Then we get a close-up of the meal she's turned down—a healthy meal of soup, bread, muffins, steak, mashed potatoes, peas, milk, and an arrangement of small disks. [8] What begins as a bad eating habit will soon develop into scoliosis, osteoporosis, or a dowager's hump. Our final caution is to follow an exercise regime; recommended sports include swinging, [9] skipping, and, presumably, power napping. ∎

As the weather cools, warmer clothes are called for.

Jerseys and sweaters...

And when it's winter, instead of wearing _one_ heavy layer of clothing...

Rubbers, to keep your feet dry.

...and change your underwear at least twice a week.

Wet shoes should not be dried near heat.

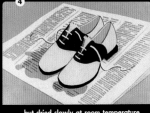
but dried slowly at room temperature.

Which of the children in the following pictures are being _sensible_ about their clothes?

YOU'RE NOT GOING OUT DRESSED LIKE THAT, ARE YOU?

and Your Clothes

Transfilms/Young America Films, 1946

It seems so basic: If it's cold, wear a sweater. If it's hot, take off the sweater. Lesson over.

But instead, hard-earned tax dollars that could have been used to, I don't know, cure polio or rebuild Europe were funneled off to pay illustrators and photographers and writers to devote their time and talent to creating carefully crafted works like this one.

And how well crafted it is. The black-and-white illustrations are gorgeous. The writing is Hemingwayesque. And the sage advice is for the ages: Change your underwear twice a week.❶ Wear rubbers.❷ Put on a jersey and tie when riding your soapbox derby racer.❸ Air-dry your saddle shoes.❹ Don't sled in a sundress.❺

And, jeepers, don't be a slob. ∎

Tom brushes his shoes every morning.

THIS IS MY BROTHER. HE LIKES TO LOOK NICE.

Right Clothes Help Health

Eye Gate Films, N.D.

Another guide to better living through clothes layering. Our stars are Tom and Betty,[1] a pair of cohabiting dolls. In the summer, they admit, they don't wear much clothing.[2] They feel cool (but look anything but) when they wear thin clothes.[3] While Tom wears shorts with knee socks (and probably takes a vicious ribbing from the boys in the schoolyard), Betty prefers playing in a Sunday-go-to-meeting dress, which she tends to rip. (Could her seamstress mommy in the bun have been the model for Anthony Perkins's mother in *Psycho*?[4]) Besides looking nice, Tom also likes to polish his shoes in the bathroom every day (just begging for a whack upside the head when Betty barrels through the door).[5]

Imagine the production of this sweet and awkward strip—grown men with meaty paws arranging the two waifs in their dollhouse set, sprinkling fake snow, and rolling up a miniature blanket on the foot of a miniature bed.[6] But at least they were in show business. ∎

This is my brother Tom. He likes to look nice.

Our summer clothes are made out of thin cloth.

We feel cool when we are dressed in our thin clothes.

When I tear my clothes, I take them to Mommy to mend.

Tom wears a raincoat and a rainhat.

In winter we wear heavy clothes to keep warm.

When it snows, I wear galoshes.

dressed

We both wear overshoes.

6

When I sleep, I put my clothes on a chair.

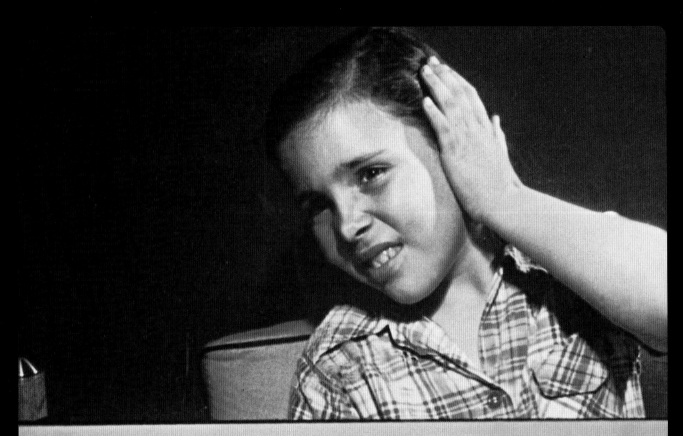

This girl has an earache. What should she do?

42

NEVER PUT ANYTHING BIGGER THAN YOUR ELBOW IN YOUR EAR

Protecting Our Eyes and Ears

Popular Science Publishing Company, Inc., 1953

After Mary turns up the television's volume full blast,❶ Mother directs her to get an education on ear and eye health from Dr. Brown, who conveniently drops by for dinner that night.❷ In the course of his discussion with Mary and her brother, John, he holds up a finger-load of earwax❸ and advises them against getting arrows and BBs in their eyes. Next we are presented with some gruesome cutaway images of dissected eyeballs,❹ then Mary is warned against being bookish.❺

I wonder if Dr. Brown was invited over for dinner often.

This lesson is also a primer on how to watch television, for people who've never done so before.❻ In 1946 there were fewer than 20,000 TV sets in the United States. The technology wasn't widely marketed until the war was over and people had the leisure time and disposable income to embrace it. By the time this strip was made, monthly TV set purchases had soared →

PROTECTING
OUR
EYES
and
EARS

One rainy afternoon Mary invited a friend to watch television.

Mary, such loud sounds may hurt you ears. Make the sound lower and mov further back.

Dr. Brown is coming here for dinner tonight
Why don't you and John ask him? 7

Dr. Brown, can you tell us how the ear works? 8

If sound is too loud, it can break the eardrum.

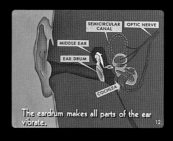

SEMICIRCULAR CANAL   OPTIC NERVE
MIDDLE EAR
EAR DRUM
COCHLEA

The eardrum makes all parts of the ear vibrate. 12

Anything placed into the ear can hurt the eardrum. Keep pins or other hard or sharp things out of your ears. 16

We may also strain our eyes while watching television. 21

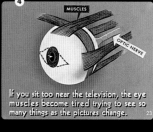

MUSCLES   OPTIC NERVE

If you sit too near the television, the eye muscles become tired trying to see so many things as the pictures change. 23

to 250,000, and the average family watched the box four to five hours a day. Two of the top three TV shows in 1953 were hosted by ukulele player Arthur Godfrey, so it was unlikely that Mary would really have trashed her hearing; it would be a few more years until rock and roll was invented to really do the trick. Top of the charts in 1953: Percy Faith, founding father of easy listening. ∎

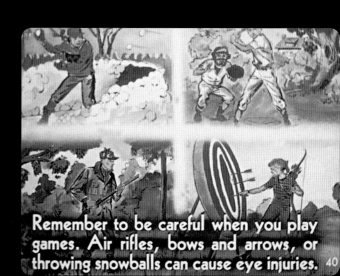

Remember to be careful when you play games. Air rifles, bows and arrows, or throwing snowballs can cause eye injuries. 40

The brown, sticky wax which forms in the outer ear is there to protect your ear. It is not dirt. 17

If you sit further back, you do not see unimportant little things. Then your eyes do not become tired. 24

Dr. Brown, Mary reads all the time. She even uses her playtime for reading. 34

Don't use your eyes too long at a time for reading or close work, Mary. Stop often and rest your eyes. 35

When you are reading a book, hold it at least a foot from the eyes. Light should fall on your book. 39

The doctor explains the anatomy of the eye and how it functions.

Only an oculist can find out what kind of glasses are best for you. 37

We decided to go in to see the dentist together. 4

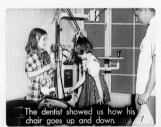
The dentist showed us how his chair goes up and down.

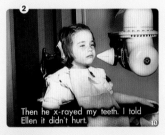
Then he x-rayed my teeth. I told Ellen it didn't hurt. 10

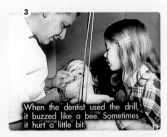
When the dentist used the drill, it buzzed like a bee. Sometimes it hurt a little bit. 13

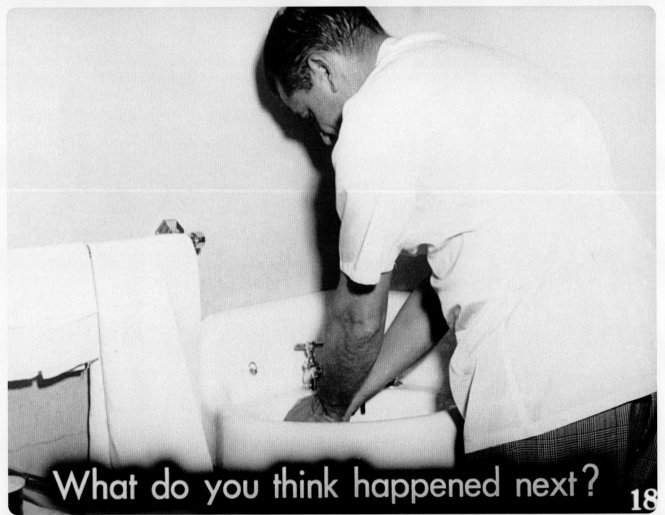

What do you think happened next? 18

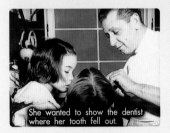
She wanted to show the dentist where her tooth fell out. 20

Then Ellen rinsed her mouth. 22

He gave us each a new tooth brush. 24

Before we left, the dentist showed us which foods help make healthy teeth. 25

We Visit the Dentist

*Key Productions/
Young America Films, 1952*

What with the dramatic lighting, the barbaric machinery, and the dentist who looks like Bela Lugosi,[1] you can't blame Ellen[2] for being a little nervous. In the 1950s, dentistry was still quite medieval. Drills vibrated and spun at a mere hundredth of the speed of today's equipment, and toothpaste with fluoride was still three years away.

Four-handed dentistry hadn't been developed to abbreviate the torture, and there were few assistants or hygienists helping the dentist bore more efficiently into your head. [3]

Mort Schindel founded Key, the fairly short-lived production company that produced this strip. He studied audiovisual techniques at Columbia Teachers' College and took courses on propaganda and mass media with famed anthropologist Margaret Mead. Soon after graduating in 1947, he founded his own company and began making films and filmstrips, which were distributed by Young America Films for the educational market. The year he made this series, he joined the U.S. Information Service and spent two years in Turkey, traveling by jeep with cameras, projectors, and generators to show and make films in remote villages that had no electricity.

In 1954, he began to develop picture-book films, in which a story was read aloud and accompanied by simple animations. Ever since, his company, Weston Woods Films, has turned many beloved favorites into short films, videos, and CD-ROMs, working with talented animators in the United States and Eastern Europe. ∎

The next time I visited my doctor, I invited Billy to come along with me.

Then Dr. Brown asked me to undress.

We watched him take a sample of my blood.

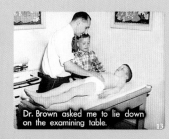

Dr. Brown asked me to lie down on the examining table.

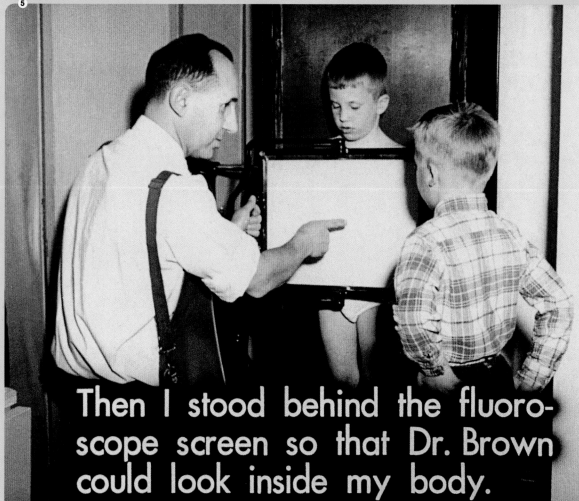

Then I stood behind the fluoroscope screen so that Dr. Brown could look inside my body.

18

Billy asked Dr. Brown to listen to his heart beat.

When we left, Billy said that now he was not afraid to visit his doctor.

The next day at school, after Billy told about our visit to the doctor, we all decided we would like to play "doctor."

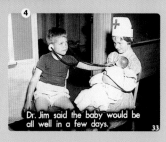

Dr. Jim said the baby would be all well in a few days.

BILLY GETS IRRADIATED

We Visit the Doctor

Key Productions/
Young America Films, 1952

Billy[1] admits to being terribly nervous about visiting the doctor, so his friend[2] invites him along to his checkup. After watching Dr. Brown[3] prick and probe his pal, Billy is cured of all his anxieties. Back at school, the kids play doctor and cure Judy's baby doll.[4]

During the examination, Billy's nameless friend stands in a fluoroscope,[5] which, as late as the 1970s, was a regular part of a child's visit to the family doctor. You'd stand against an X-ray machine and radiation would pass through your body so light and shadow could be projected onto a fluorescent screen. Instead of the static picture of an X-ray, the doctor saw a live, moving picture of your young innards. (As we see in this strip, he also shielded himself with a lead apron while his young patients stood around unprotected.) And instead of a swift burst of radiation, you'd be subjected to a steady stream, often fifty to one hundred times the dose used today.

Before researchers discovered its many dangers, radiation exposure was a regular part of life. You were X-rayed in the womb as part of your mother's abdominal exam, then again as a newborn (for "preventive" reasons). In the 1950s, buses loaded with primitive and leaking X-ray machines were sent to schools nationwide, conducting mass screenings for TB. Acne and freckles were zapped with the beauty shop's radiation machine. And most shoe stores were fitted with fluoroscopes to penetrate your shoes and bones to reveal how your new saddle shoes fit your growing feet. You and your mom probably escaped unharmed, but woe to the hapless shoe clerks who ran the deadly machines every day. It wasn't until the mid-1960s that fluoroscopes were finally banned from shoe stores. ■

"Open up wide," said the doctor.

"WE'LL HAVE YOU FEELING FINE SOON"

Workers for Health

Curriculum Films, early 1950s

After Bruce[1] is absent because of illness one too many times, his teacher turns him in. He and his mother meet with the school doctor,[2] who hands him over to Bruce's family doctor for "treatment."[3] Bruce is ordered to bed for a week, where he keeps himself very busy[4] so as not to disturb his neglectful mother, gets well enough to fight with his sister,[5] and goes back to school, fit as a fiddle.[6]

Despite a lousy title and some shaky logic (the only thing Bruce's doctor seems to prescribe is the very bed rest that got Bruce in trouble in the first place), *Workers for Health* is a friendly and realistic strip that makes health care professionals seem concerned and involved. ■

Bruce's seat is empty.
He is sick in bed.

Later Bruce came back to school.
He wasn't feeling well.

The nurse gave him a note
for his mother, asking her
to come in with Bruce.

Bruce and his mother came to the school doctor.

Then he turned to Bruce. "We'll have you feeling fine soon."

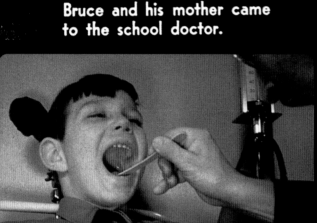

Bruce opened up wide, because he wanted to help the doctor.

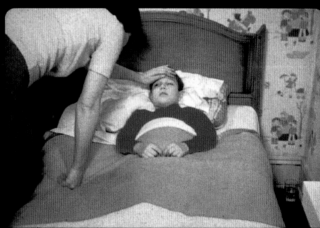

Mother put Bruce to bed.

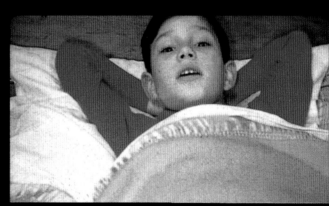

The next week Bruce felt fine. "The doctors knew what to do!" Bruce said.

"Bruce needs some treatment.
Take him to your own doctor.
He'll take care of Bruce."

He kept himself busy, because
he knew mother was busy.

"I can't fight with you now,"
Bruce said. "I must rest
if I am to get well."

... or exploring the rim of a glass of milk.

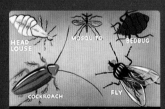

...a mosquito, cockroach, bedbug, head louse, fly. Just five insects.

But — in your home they are a danger to your health.

Mosquitoes are a nuisance! Scratching their itching bites may cause infection

Cockroaches are a kitchen pest whose dirty habits may spread disease.

...and spray the bed and mattress with a bedbug killer.

If you have head lice, wash your hair with a special soap,...

The fly lives on filth and lays its eggs there.

❶ REMEMBER, INSECT CONTROL IS A NATIONAL, A COMMUNITY, AND A PERSONAL PROBLEM. DO YOUR PART.

BUGS ARE NOT YOUR FRIENDS

Insect Pests and Disease

Transfilms/
Young America Films, 1946

Gross insects lurk everywhere, spreading all sorts of disease, and it's our duty to wipe them out with flyswatters and sprays. This strip seems to still be under the spell of wartime propaganda, what with its dire warnings [1] and exclamation points to mobilize the youth of America to fight these dreaded enemies.

A couple of years before, the first weapon of mass destruction arrived to level the battlefield. A Swiss chemist named Paul Muller invented DDT, a discovery so fantastic that in 1948 it earned him the Nobel Prize. Back in its day, DDT was considered a miracle because it killed all sorts of bugs but was "barely" toxic to mammals and didn't break down in the environment or wash away in the rain. And it was dirt cheap.

People began to sterilize their homes and workplaces, indiscriminately spraying gallons of DDT everywhere. The results were wonderful: Crop yield soared, and malaria came under control as mosquitoes vanished. DDT trucks rumbled through neighborhoods on summer evenings, spraying anything and anyone in their path. Children ran out to play in the lovely cool spray.

It took twenty years for the piper to arrive for payment, but eventually tenacious DDT residue started to show up everywhere—people got sick, and birds, animals, and plants started dying off. Meanwhile, new generations of insects grew resistant to the chemicals, and tougher, more toxic ones had to be developed.

All in all, eradicating so-called pests was an arrogant crusade for which we—and our environment—are still paying a heavy price. Should have stuck with the swatter. ∎

Would you know how to make a boat out of this?

16

PARTY HATS ARE ALWAYS NEEDED

Making Things with Paper

Filmstrip-of-the-Month Club, 1959

This is a lovely filmstrip, and somebody seems to have had a lot of fun creating it. It teaches children that you need strong paper to make cups [1] and that swans are good table decorations. [2] It's full of useful tips—how to fold pleats and something called "the catsteps" [3] and how to turn a paper hat into a boat [4] or a basket. [5] These are the sorts of "Life Adjustment" lessons that would make you a hit at birthday parties throughout your life, certainly more so than learning about the Louisiana Purchase or the distance to Mars.

Still, truth be told, one would have to be a fairly inept art teacher to resort to occupying an elementary school class with a filmstrip, even one so charming as *Making Things with Paper*. ■

Just look at this table covered with the many things these children have made out of paper for their party. ③

There are room decorations, part hats, a cup, a basket and a doll fo a puppet show.

these are other things they used

brass fasteners

Stapler

hole Puncher

scissors

Colored Paper

ruler

Paul made a different decoration with the pleat fold. Have you another idea? Why not make it? ⑨

In making another decoration, a strip of paper was used. ⑩

Party hats are always needed. Some are called toy soldiers' hats. Some are decorated . . . ⑭

NURSE

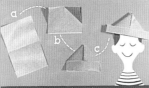
. . . some are made with newspaper; some with wrapping paper; some with colored paper. ⑮

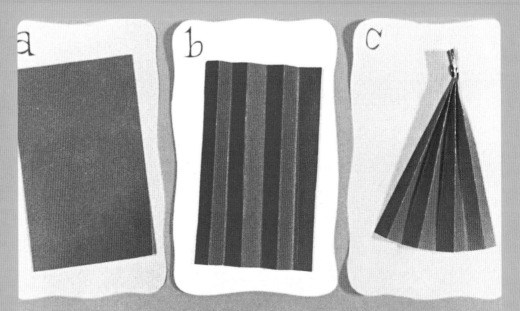
5

What could you add to it to make it a basket? Would you decorate the baskets? ⑱

1

Cups were easy to make. The children used THE RIGHT KIND OF PAPER. They chose a strong paper. ⑲

a   b   c

One of the room decorations was made from the pleat fold. ⑦

Here are other strip decorations. Many strips were used to make them. ⑪

3 Ann discovered that two strips of different colors folded in a certain way made an interesting hanging. This is called the catsteps. ⑫

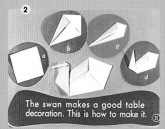

2

The swan makes a good table decoration. This is how to make it. ㉑

Children's THEATER

These are two puppets that will be used in a play. ㉒

In making this interesting boy puppet. Remember the catsteps for arms and legs?

Paper
Crayons
snow
bead
Staples
Paper Strips
Boy

The children invited their parents to the party. They made their own invitations. ㉓

this is another hat you can make

a   b   c   d

e

f

⑰

SOCIAL STUDIES

SOCIAL STUDIES

Let's ride our time machine back a half century or so for a little attitude adjustment. America had gone through a decade of the Great Depression. So had the world. Economies were trashed, farms went bust, and people were pretty ambivalent about institutions and authorities and the future. Next up: another decade of world war and its aftermath. Plans were put on hold, enormous sacrifices were made, and millions and millions of people were killed.

Things didn't return to normal just because bombs were dropped on Hiroshima and Nagasaki. World War II wasn't quite the John Wayne epic we think of now: Nazis and Japanese and GIs emptying machine guns at each other so they could take over the world. It was the end of a chapter stretching back forty years in which history, politics, culture, and economics were rewritten. Now a new page had been turned, but it was still blank. The balance of power around the planet had been turned on its head. Europe was a smoking ruin, and nations that had been the cream of civilization were now back in the Stone Age. Every continent was profoundly affected. New countries and borders and systems of government were popping up in every corner.

America's very character had been altered. Through the Depression and the war, class distinctions had been diminished, and people had come to value communalism. But without a common enemy, that spirit drifted down into conformity and conservatism. Americans yearned for order and predictability. They were suspicious of anyone who was different and attempted to stray from the herd. They were afraid of social disorder—divorce, juvenile delinquency, black people, and beatniks—and lived in dread that the Soviets would also be tempted to use the Bomb.

The economy was unclogged after a dozen or more years of torpor: The Gross National Product almost tripled from 1940 to 1960. New industries, companies, products, services, and jobs gushed forth and created a new middle-class materialism. Suddenly they wanted—and could have—convertibles, telephones, televisions, and electrical appliances, too.

Japan: Mrs. Okamoto serves rice from the big wooden bucket and soup from a kettle behind it. They have meat twice a month. **39**

Our vanquished foes.
From *People Are People,* page 91

Women had a new outlook. During all the years their men were far away at war, they had been self-sufficient breadwinners. After the war, most left the workplace and went back to their kitchens, becoming housewives again—but their expectations and perspectives were changed forever.

Men had changed too. More than a million went on to college courtesy of the GI Bill. The war had fathered the development of many new technologies, and postindustrial America needed droves of educated, technical white-collar workers. By the mid 1950s, corporate managers, teachers, salesmen, and office workers outnumbered the blue-collar workforce.

America's landscape was being redrawn. Subsidized mortgages and a high birthrate fueled a boom in housing. Millions of new homes and gigantic shopping centers began to spring up, and the suburbs were born. Small towns were transformed as the new national Interstate highways bypassed them or suddenly swelled their ranks. People swarmed to the West, and the Sun Belt exploded.

America's educational system reflected all this change, most notably in the social studies curriculum. Everyone's dad had been abroad, had seen the world through rifle sights; now kids had to learn about a world at peace and what sorts of relationships this country should have with former allies and enemies. Everyone's parents had stories of privation; now children needed to see the country from a positive, productive perspective, where everyone pulled together to build the world's strongest economy. Law and order were vital as well. Sure, we had bomb shelters in our backyards and were electrocuting Commie spies, but kids could rest assured that broad-shouldered policemen were there to protect all law-abiding citizens.

The world was different. We were different. Everything was different. And yet filmstrips could reduce all that change into a series of neat little rectangles that would stream light through the chaos and explain it all. ∎

Africa: The Zamba Alumas, of Lujulu, where every girl's first daily task is to gather leaves for her skirt. 5

FOREIGNERS CAN'T HELP IT

**People Are People
the World Over**

Curriculum Films, 1949

This strip profiles a dozen families from very different parts of the world, a world that in 1949 had been carved up and was being rebuilt by the United States and the Allies. It begins by stating a noble sentiment: ". . . regardless of these differences . . . 'people are people the world over.'" Nonetheless, the lesson is riddled with bias and racism.

First we go to Lujulu, Sudan, to meet the Zamba Alumas. [1] From them we learn that bare-breasted girls' "first daily task is to gather leaves for their skirts." Next in China (remember, this is in 1949, the year of Mao's revolution), we meet the Ho Fu-yuans, [2] who "would not let their little girl be photographed for fear of evil spirits." In Germany, we see the Stieglitzes, [3] "who married the year Hitler came to power" (a not-so-subtle reminder of the Nazi past). Pakistan, a brand-new country just months old, is represented by the hopelessly heathen Mohammed Usmans, [4] "who had not met before their wedding." Italy features the Guercinis, [5] "whose clean house is painted yellow because the neighbors' houses are red." (Is this caption intentionally surreal, or are their neighbors all Communists? Or do the Guercinis tend to lose their way a lot?) ➔

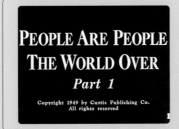

PEOPLE ARE PEOPLE
THE WORLD OVER
Part 1

Copyright 1949 by Curtis Publishing Co.
All rights reserved

China: The Ho Fu-yuans, of Kia-ting, who would not let their little girl be photographed, for fear of evil spirits.

Germany: The Stieglitzes, of Wollau, w married the year Hitler came to power

Pakistan: The Mohammed Usmans, of Patni, who had not met before their wedding. **8**

In Pakistan they grow rice and have dried dates and *chappatis* for lunch.

England: The Hiatts, of Hook Norton, who like to read Western stories. **9**

Italy: The Guercinis, of Greve, whose clean house is painted yellow because the neighbors' houses are red. **10**

France: The Redouins, of Fossés, who sent messages by carrier pigeon to England during the German occupation of France. **11**

The French eat their lunch under a barnyard tree. They lost last year's winter-wheat crop but are making ends meet.

92

Next up, the Redouins, **6** French folk "who sent messages by carrier pigeon to England during the German occupation"—in other words, they're not collaborators and deserve to be in an American filmstrip. The Japanese, **7** however, are just ridiculous bureaucratic buffoons. The Okamotos have to pay "a cow tax and a *supplementary* cow tax" and eat rice out of a big bucket. No wonder we beat them.

The Mexican Gonzalezes **8** are cockfighting primitives, and the el Gamels **9** of Egypt have donkeys descended from those in the Bible (which they themselves don't believe in, being unchristian). Finally, the Baloghs, **10** unregenerate Czechoslovakian party animals who collaborated with the Jerrys and ended up behind the iron curtain for their troubles. They consider wolf meat a delicacy.

By contrast, we have the Hiatts **11** of Hook Norton, England, who "like to read Western stories" (i.e., they love the U.S. of A.), and the Pratts **12** of Iowa, who have a big shiny tractor and a cute nine-year-old daughter who "would rather ride her pony bareback than do anything else."

People may be people all over the world, but in 1949, most of the folks in this strip were dealing with five years of near-apocalyptic war and dislocation, the result of xenophobia, racism, and imperialism. This strip indoctrinates a new generation to believe that other people are superstitious, primitive, and very foreign.

The beautiful photos, by the way, are not tainted by the captions that accompany them. They were excerpted from a *Ladies Home Journal* article by the great Magnum photo editor John G. Morris. Ironically, Magnum was founded on the belief that the role of photojournalism was to provoke us into a new awareness of what is happening in the world. ∎

Egypt: The el Gamels, of Manayel Shebein el Kanater, whose donkeys are descended from those in the Bible. **12**

The el Gamel boys are trained to sit straight and keep quiet at the table.

Japan: The Okamotos, of Oshika, whose twelve annual taxes include a cow tax and a *supplementary* cow tax. **13**

United States: The Pratts, of Iowa, whose nine-year-old daughter would rather ride her pony bareback than do anything else. **14**

Mexico: The Gonzalezes, of Moravatio, where cockfights are legal and it is the custom to "steal" a bride. **15**

Czechoslovakia: The Baloghs, of Furolac, where weddings last three days and wolf meat is considered a delicacy. **16**

From *Lowland Indians*, Curriculum Films, 1958

SOUTH AMERICANS ARE OUR AMIGOS

Amazon Village

Curriculum Films, 1958

This strip depicts the Amazonians as cheery, industrious churchgoers whose government provides them with medical programs and education. Gotta love them, and you were supposed to do just that.

The strip is a product of undiluted government-sponsored propaganda programs. In 1941, as part of his so-called Good Neighbor Policy, FDR established the office of Coordinator of Inter-American Affairs (CIAA, the agency was eventually absorbed into the Department of State) to make sure that Latin America would remain squarely in the American camp once we entered the war. That solidarity was encouraged by economic development; by U.S. withdrawal from Cuba, Haiti, Bolivia, and Mexico; and by building bonds of friendship through cultural exchange and education. ➔

95

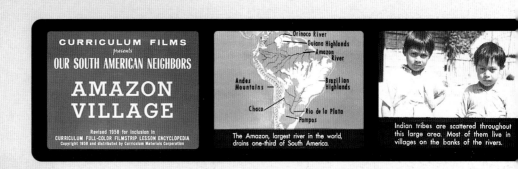

CURRICULUM FILMS
presents
OUR SOUTH AMERICAN NEIGHBORS
AMAZON VILLAGE
Revised 1958 for inclusion in
CURRICULUM FULL-COLOR FILMSTRIP LESSON ENCYCLOPEDIA
Copyright 1958 and distributed by Curriculum Materials Corporation

Orinoco River
Guiana Highlands
Amazon River
Andes Mountains
Brazilian Highlands
Chaco
Rio de la Plata
Pampas

The Amazon, largest river in the world, drains one-third of South America.

Indian tribes are scattered throughout this large area. Most of them live in villages on the banks of the rivers.

hout
e in
s.

The huts have no windows or doors.
The floors are dirt.

The thatched roof protects the Indians
from the hot sun and the heavy rains.

The Indians drink river water, and use
the river for washing and bathing.

Rice and mandioca are the main foods.
When rice is ready to be used, it is
put in a large wooden mortar.

96

When Nelson Rockefeller was named head of the CIAA, he got in touch with Julien Bryan, who had made acclaimed documentary films about the Soviet Union in the early1930s and had been nominated for an Oscar for his film on the Warsaw blitzkrieg. Bryan was contracted to make films on Latin American culture for American schools and a matching set on the U.S. for export to Latin America. His photographs were also turned into a series of filmstrips called *Our South American Neighbors.* These landmark films are still in distribution.

Bryan went on to produce and direct many other ethnographic films designed to promote peace and harmony and greater understanding among the peoples of the world. He and his son, Sam, made films about Melanesia, Mali, Japan, and Afghanistan, all portraits of everyday life in nonurban communities around the world. Bryan died in 1974. ■

The government sends a doctor to the village to help fight malaria and other tropical diseases.

The rice is pounded with a wooden pestle.

Children help to work the paste into flat cakes that are baked in ovens.

On holidays all the villagers go to a fiesta—a big party and dance.

All children in this Amazon village go to school.

The school was built by the government. The teacher came from a nearby village.

When Sunday comes, the villagers travel by oxcart or walk to a nearby village.

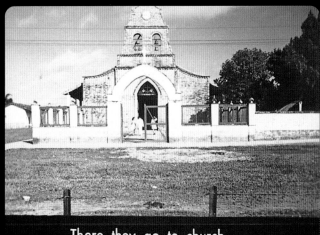
There they go to church.

Maybe your mother buys her milk at the store.
Sometimes milk comes in a paper carton.

GOT CHOLESTEROL?

The Story of Milk

Society for Visual Education,
ca. 1955

This strip follows the production chain from cow to farm to receiving station to bottling plant to the milkman who delivers to your door. (Remember that? Me neither). It was shot documentary style on location with the assistance of Quaker Oats, the National Dairy Council, and the Ful-O-Pep Research Farm, and it verges on propaganda for the dairy industry.

What's the big deal about cow's milk and why have we always been encouraged to drink so much of it? Well, in 1912, vitamin A was discovered in cow's milk and egg yolks and seemed to be key to animal growth and to promoting good health in humans, too. The government immediately got behind the cause and promoted the protective wonders of butter, buttermilk, whole milk, eggs, and the ever-struggling farmer. The dairy industry was the immediate benefactor. ➜

The Story of MILK CREAM

Have you ever thought about how you get your glass of milk?

Milk is made up of things that you need to help you grow.

Dairy cows must be kept very clean. The barn must be kept clean, too. Do you know why?

Modern dairy farmers save time by using milking machines.

The milkhouse is a separate building. The milk is kept cold here in a bulk tank.

Large tank trucks, like this one, carry the milk to the city pasteurizing plants.

The cows eat feed made from corn and dried grass and press their mouths into drinking cups to get water.

To make sure American milk wasn't watered down and robbed of the benefits of dairy fat, milk was priced according to its fat content—the more fat you bought, the less you paid. Similarly, discriminatory regulations were passed against the sale of margarine. To protect and promote the health of all Americans (particularly the ones in the dairy industry), the government provided subsidies, agreeing to buy all leftover inventories from the farmers. Those inventories of milk, butter, and cheese would be distributed to soldiers, prisoners—and schoolchildren. For the next thirty-five years, we were fed a lot of butter and drank a lot of milk.

During the late 1950s, scientists began to link dairy fat with high blood cholesterol and the risk of heart disease. Doctors performing autopsies on slain Korean and American soldiers discovered that the arteries of 75 percent of the young GIs were beginning to be constricted by atherosclerotic deposits. The Koreans, who ate a far more vegetarian diet, had none.

As other studies linking animal fat with heart disease and stroke emerged, nutritionists issued new guidelines. Yet Americans, despite being drilled with these dietary lessons since elementary school, continue to consume far more meat and dairy foods than any other people on earth, and stroke and heart attacks remain among our most common causes of death.

One guess why. ∎

This is a pasteurizing and bottling plant. Sometime, you might visit one.

The milk is pumped from the trucks into holding tanks, like these, inside the dairy.

Milk is given many tests. Here it is tested for butterfat content.

Have you ever seen any of these trucks when you were on a trip?

The milk is bottled, capped, and inspected before it is sent off for delivery.

Here is your milk, delivered fresh, pure, and cold to you.

Mother uses milk and milk products in her baking and cooking.

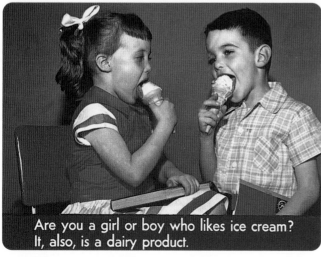

Are you a girl or boy who likes ice cream? It, also, is a dairy product.

Chickens, ducks, and turkeys come from poultry farms.

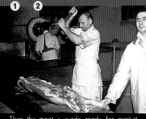
Then the meat is made ready for market.

Trimming sides of bacon.

These workers are packaging sliced meats.

The butcher shop was very clean.

Paul learned that T-bone, sirloin, and tenderloin steaks are the best cuts of beef.

The butcher put a piece of beef into a large grinder. Paul saw that hamburgers are made of ground beef.

Paul saw how a machine was used for slicing cold cuts.

Paul went into the big refrigerator in which the meat was kept.

LET'S MEET MEAT

The Butcher   Before the advent of things like McNuggets, fruit
Eye Gate, 1950s   rollups, and popcorn chicken, people were more
in touch with the origins of their food. This filmstrip is quite explicit
about how living, furry animals are slaughtered and chopped up so
we can eat them.

We go behind the scenes at a meatpacking plant ❶ and see butchers wielding axes ❷
unapologetically turning carcasses into bologna and bacon. ❸ Paul's butcher ❹ gives him a lesson
on origins of various cuts of meat, then machetes some T-bones ❺ and grinds up a herd of
burgers. ❻ After the carnage, Paul takes his grim package of meat home, ❼ wondering if he should
become a vegan. ■

Paul thanked the butcher and took his package of meat home.

THE POSTMAN ALWAYS BRINGS TWICE

Post Office Workers

Curriculum Films, early 1950s

Long before faxes, E-mail, bar codes, and FedEx became commonplace, the U.S. mail was extremely dependable. In fact, when this filmstrip was produced, mailmen even delivered twice every day to virtually every home in the country. But like all things American, the mail changed. By the 1960s, 80 percent of it was business related: Bills, checks, and advertising replaced personal correspondence in our mailboxes. To organize this growing avalanche of paper, the zip code was introduced in 1963.

When this strip was produced, most mail traveled by rail; some ten thousand trains traversed the country around the clock in the 1930s, but after World War II the rail system declined rapidly. Trucks and planes became increasingly important links in the chain of communication.

In 1959, the U.S. Post Office even attempted to incorporate guided missiles into its delivery system, test-firing one loaded with three thousand letters at Mayport, Florida. The service boasted, "Before man reaches the moon, mail will be delivered within hours from New York to California, to Britain, to India or Australia by guided missiles." Sadly, ICBMs were reserved for other, less postal duties. ■

CURRICULUM FILMS, INC.
presents
COMMUNITY WORKERS
Post Office Workers
SECOND REVISED EDITION
Distributed by CURRICULUM FILMS, INC.

Bruce went to the post office to send a present to Bobbie.

"The package is well wrapped," said the clerk.

The clerk weighed the package.
He printed a stamp to paste on it.

"That will cost twelve cents."
Bruce gave him a quarter.

He had to reach to get
to the opening.

A man separated the letters.
All the letters for one town
were put in one bag.

The bag goes into a truck, which
goes to a train, which goes to
Bobbie's town.

A truck took the bags
to the town's post office.

"I wonder what's in it,"
said Bobbie.

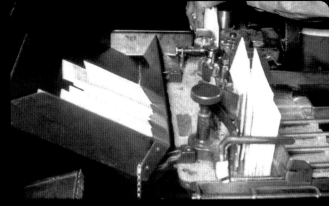

A machine cancelled the stamps
so they couldn't be used again.

The letters were separated.
The mail-man put the letters
in the order of the houses.

His bag was heavy.

Bobbie opened the box.
"What a lot of wrapping!"

"Oh, boy! What a surprise!"

Policemen are brave and smart.

"I WANT TO BE A POLICEMAN"

Larry Helps the Police

Curriculum Films, ca.1950

At the beginning of this cautionary tale, we meet Larry's dad, a square-jawed patrolman[1] whose seven-year-old son[2] idolizes him. He became a policeman by doing many things in a black turtleneck:[3] He studied the law in huge, yellowing, leather-bound books,[4] then crouched over a supine African American man who seems to be napping,[5] caressing his ribs in what is purportedly first aid. Next comes a fight scene [6] straight out of *Seven Brides for Seven Brothers* and a fantastic image in which Dad threatens the photographer with a Saturday night special.[7] →

CURRICULUM FILMS, INC.
presents
COMMUNITY WORKERS
Larry Helps the Police
SECOND REVISED EDITION
Distributed by CURRICULUM FILMS, INC.

[1]

Larry's father is a policeman. Larry is proud of his father.

[3] [4]

He learned the laws. Then he became a policeman.

He learned to use fingerprints
to find criminals.

He learned first-aid.

He learned how to shoot.

He learned how to fight.

After these thrills, Larry wanders off alone ⑧ and witnesses a hit-and-run accident.⑨ A man ⑩ dressed just like Larry has been nailed by a beautiful woody station wagon,⑪ which then careens away through a red light. Despite having both sets of wheels roll over him, the victim is able to get back on his pins with a little help from the seven-year-old. A passing cop happens on the scene, gets the woody's license number from Larry, and calls the precinct.⑫

Within a few frames, the culprit is busted. We never see his face, but he appears, head bowed contritely, before the desk sergeant, who apparently functions as judge and jury, too.⑬ After justice is swiftly dispensed,⑭ the budding crime stopper drops by the station and gets a handshake from his idol.⑮

Larry Helps the Police was designed to give children a sense of security. Like today, the early 1950s were nervous times. Nazis and Japanese bombers were still fresh memories, and the ➜

Larry said, "I want to be a policeman!"

"Meanwhile help the police by keeping yourself safe."

Larry crossed the street
the right way. He was safe.

He reached the other side.
Someone was hit by a car.

Larry ran to help.

He told the policemen
the license number.

112

Larry came to the police station.
"Good work!" said his father.

They arrested the driver.

The driver went to court.
He was punished.

Communist menace lurked in every corner. Still, Larry could walk down the street by himself without fear of ending up with his face on a milk carton. That army of stern but caring cops with shining brass buttons was always around to watch over him.

In the 1950s, the public's view of the police was epitomized by Andy Griffith of Mayberry, a nice guy who wore a badge and didn't need a gun. But that was before the march on Selma, before the 1968 Democratic Convention in Chicago, long before Rodney King and Abner Louima.

By the 1960s, crime began to escalate. The police got off the beat and into squad cars, making them increasingly remote from the communities they patrolled and far less available to give directions and help kids cross the street. By the time Larry was a teenager, his friends would likely have begun to use the new term for law enforcement: *pig*.

This gripping story has the typical look of a Curriculum Film, with off-the-street casting, solid composition, and lush, Douglas Sirk color. Still, it's as wooden as the station wagon's doors, and even a second grader can tell the whole thing is totally staged. ∎

Bulldozers are strong.
They clear the way.   1

Bulldozers push or pull.
They move piles of dirt.   3

Bulldozers are tractors.
Tractors pull machines
that scoop up dirt.   4

Tractors pull the load of dirt.
The dirt is carried away.   5

Scrapers have long blades.
Scrapers make the road level.   6

Trucks dump tar and gravel.
The gravel is spread on the road.   7

Finishers spread asphalt.
Asphalt makes good roads.   8

Steam rollers are heavy.
They make roads even.   9

Mixer trucks carry concrete.
They mix the concrete as they go.   10

The mixer truck travels.
The concrete is ready
when the trip is over.   11

Sweepers keep our streets clean.
The small broom sweeps the dirt
out from the curb.   12

The big broom sweeps the dirt
into the hopper.   13

Machines clear the snow.
The snow goes into the truck.   14

The truck carries water.
It washes the streets.
It keeps the streets clean.   15

Roads need to be fixed.
Air drills break up pavement.   16

Clam shovels pick up dirt.
Clam shovels pick up rock.
They load dirt and rock in trucks.   17

Clam shovels are strong.
They lift heavy loads.   18

Bucket shovels dig up dirt.
The dirt is dropped into trucks.   20

Hoe shovels dig dirt.
The bucket is like a hoe.   21

Dragline shovels carry sand.
The bucket dumps the sand.   23

BULLDOZERS ARE STRONG, STEAM ROLLERS ARE HEAVY

Road Builders at Work

Curriculum Films, 1950

The heavy equipment in this strip wasn't just rebuilding America's roads. It was rebuilding America itself. In 1950, there were very few highways, and traveling across the country could take a month or two on bumpy, poorly paved roads. At the same time, there was a postwar flood of new-car buying, and with the chill of the cold war and the burgeoning anxiety about nuclear attack, many felt that it was vital to develop a modern interstate highway system to allow cities to be evacuated and military gear to move quickly.

President Eisenhower pushed for a plan to build a system of forty-two thousand miles of linked modern highways, the world's largest public works project. In 1956, one of the first stretches of the interstate opened in Topeka, Kansas. The project, which took thirty-five years to complete, radically changed American life, creating congestion, suburban sprawl, and smog, and smothering small towns and mass transport.

The interstate has eradicated many regional differences, transformed commerce and manufacturing, and makes America more efficient and less interesting with every passing year. Instead of driving *through* places and seeing the landscape, and the differences between one community and the next, we now drive *to* places, zipping down the highway, seeing little more than others' bumpers and signs listing the chains of fast-food joints and gas stations at the exits. There's nothing to see out the window. Thank goodness we have onboard DVD players.

It's ironic that though we think of the 1950s as a time of cultural conservatism and conformity, in many ways America today is far more homogenous. The interstate helped make us a coast-to-coast strip mall. ■

LET'S LEARN ABOUT ILLEGAL IMMIGRATION

At first glance, this filmstrip evokes one of the greatest movies of all time. The photography, subject matter, and the period foreshadow *On the Waterfront*, Elia Kazan's stirring 1954 tale of corruption and heroism on the docks of Hoboken, New Jersey. These images could have come from the location scout for the movie, and you can easily imagine Marlon Brando wandering through the scene saying, "I coulda had class! I coulda been a contender."

Closer scrutiny reveals that the filmstrip is preoccupied with a different sort of dirty rat from the ones in the movie. There are creepy images of men in gas masks, [1] huge heaps of poison, [2] an abandoned lone child and baggage, [3] and bureaucrats checking papers. [4] Four years after VJ day, the specter of threat and war still hangs over "the Harbor."

In 1949, New York harbor was a bustling place: Half a million passengers arrived by ocean liner; steam paddleboats and ferryboats worked the Hudson River; twenty million tons of cargo landed on its docks. But the port was in decline, plagued by corruption and losing out to other ports on the eastern seaboard, and it would take Brando and Karl Malden to straighten things out. ∎

THE HARBOR

A HARBOR is more than just a refuge for ships. 1

Large incoming ships are met at the entrance of the harbor by a *pilot boat*.

A *harbor* *pilot* comes aboard... 4

...to steer the ship safely to its pier. 5

Persons with contagious disease are removed to the *Quarantine Station*.

The *Immigration Service* checks

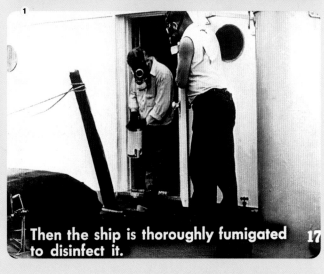

DANGER
POISON CUP
CONTAINS
DEADLY RAT POISON
DO NOT HANDLE

Rat poison is placed around the ship. 16

Then the ship is thoroughly fumigated to disinfect it. 17

If the ship is from a foreign port, a doctor from the _Quarantine Service_ also comes aboard. 6

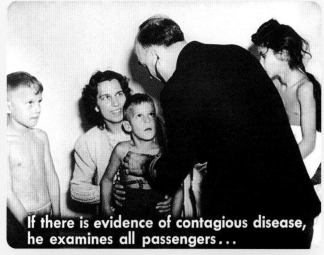

If there is evidence of contagious disease, he examines all passengers...

This young fellow is minding his family's baggage until... 13

..._Customs Service_ men inspect it for items that are taxable or against the law to bring into the country. 14

The _Coast Guard_ patrols the harbor to enforce navigation and safety laws. 28

In some harbors there are _police boats_... 30

Buses go where trains can't go.
They go where streetcars can't go.
Buses do not need tracks.

1

ODE TO RALPH KRAMDEN

Buses at Work

Curriculum Films, 1950

In 1950, Americans were shaking off the privations of war, building roads, buying cars, and moving out of the cities and small towns to spanking new suburbs.

Privately owned bus companies soon felt the pinch. The Fifth Avenue Coach Company, whose beautiful double-decker we see parked by Greenwich Village's Washington Square arch,❶ began to service the city in 1897. By 1962, it was gone. In cities across the country, subsidized public transportation made it increasingly difficult for private bus companies to compete. More significantly, new suburbanites were acquiring new cars, and the bus companies found it impossible to profitably serve their sprawling and dispersed communities. Just as this filmstrip arrived in schools, local governments began to take over the privately owned transit companies.

Intercity bus lines (Greyhound❷ was one) had been around since the turn of the last century. As more and better roads were built, new companies joined the competition, and by ➜

CURRICULUM FILMS *presents* TRANSPORTATION (For Primary Grades) BUSES AT WORK SECOND REVISED EDITION Copyright MCML and Distributed by CURRICULUM FILMS, INC.

Passengers wait in the bus station.

Tickets are sold in the station. Tickets are sold at windows.

The baggage is put on the bus. 4

The driver checks the tickets
as the passengers get on the bus. 5

The seats are deep and soft.
The seats tip back.
The passengers can rest. 6

The bus stops.
Passengers can eat.
Passengers can rest. 7

the mid 1920s there were thousands of independent lines running between towns. The business hit its peak during the war years and unraveled soon after. As more people bought their own cars and took to flying in airplanes, the long-distance bus haul became the choice only of those of limited means. Few companies besides Greyhound survived.

The sole success story seems to be the school bus. **❸** Even though it looks pretty much as it did in 1950, today's version is safer, better driven, and better maintained than ever. In 2005, almost a half million public school buses will carry twenty-four million students a total of four billion miles. So sit quietly, no spitballs, and don't put your hands out the window. ■

A taxi is a bus.
A taxi carries only
a few passengers. 20

Buses are washed at the yard.
Buses are cleaned at the yard. 8

Buses are kept at the yard.
Buses are filled with gasoline.
Buses are filled with oil. 10

Bus drivers go to school.
They learn to drive safely. 11

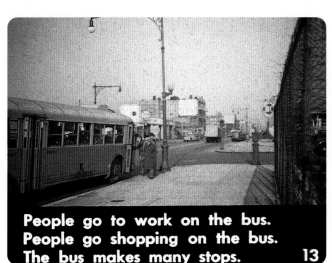

People go to work on the bus.
People go shopping on the bus.
The bus makes many stops. 13

Some city buses have two floors. 16

Ambulances are buses.
Ambulances carry passengers
who cannot sit up. 22

Children ride in buses.
The buses carry them to school. 23

People live in trailers. 4

DON'T TRASH TRAILERS

Trailers at Work
Curriculum Films, 1950

Though this strip brims with strange and beautiful images, *Trailers* seems a strange subject for a school lesson. Its subtext is the dynamic and productive new spirit reinvigorating postwar America. Goods are being manufactured and hauled everywhere, new cars are rolling off the line for the first time in half a decade,❶ people are hitting brand-new roads in search of adventures,❷ dentists in rolling, motorized offices are fixing teeth.❸ Trailers are at work, and so is the nation.

But the loveliest frames in the strip are of vacation trailers, particularly that aluminum bullet, the Airstream Clipper, the first trailer based on modern aircraft design. Its ultraefficient interiors❹ are of polished wood, with perfect little sinks and hideaway beds, every detail urging the viewer to head for the horizon and seek America.

Incidentally, of all the Airstreams built since the early 1930s, more than 60 percent are still rolling down America's highways. ■

CURRICULUM FILMS
presents
TRANSPORTATION
(For Primary Grades)

TRAILERS AT WORK
Copyright MCML and Distributed by
CURRICULUM FILMS, INC.
SECOND REVISED EDITION

Trailers have no motors.
Trailers must be pulled.   1

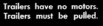

Cars pull trailers.
Jeeps pull trailers.
Trailers are vacation homes.

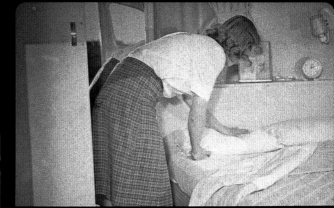

People sleep in trailers.
The seats can be made into beds. 6

s. 2

People travel in trailers.
They pull their homes with them. 3

Trailers have running water.
People can wash their hands. 5

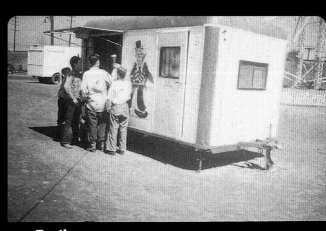

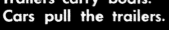

Trailers carry boats.
Cars pull the trailers. 8

Trailers are stores.
They can be moved around. 10

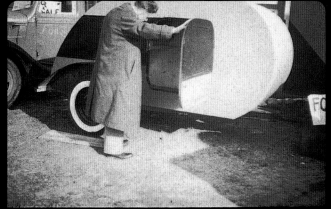

Some trailers are small.
There is room for a bed. 7

Trucks pull big trailers.
Trailers move furniture.
They go on long trips. 12

Trailers carry cars.
Cars drive on the trailer. 17

What pulls big trailers? 25

What will this trailer carry? 27

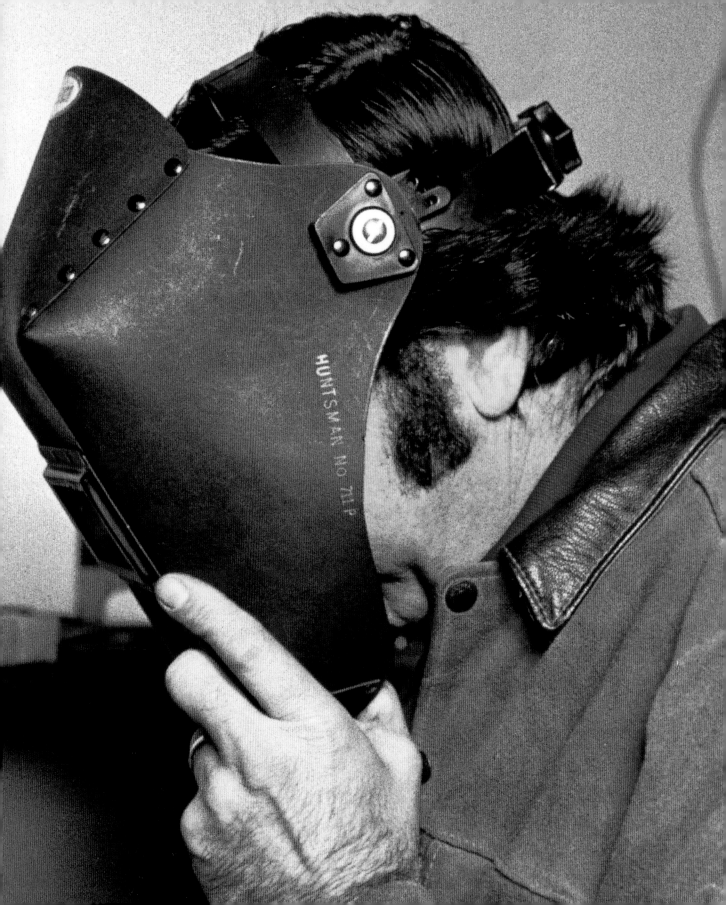

ZIP GUN 101

Welder,[1] So you think you want to be a welder. But do
Machinist,[2] you know what the job entails? Do you have
Foundry Worker[3] what it takes? Have you paid attention during

Audiotronics Corporation, 1970 your math and mechanical drawing classes?
Do you look good in a mask?

These filmstrips were part of a series designed to help students explore careers in "Industrial Arts" such as metalworking. They reviewed exciting topics—the five major methods of casting, the process of resistance welding, the way to operate a boring machine (and we're not talking about our filmstrip projector). We get to see stimulating action photos of micrometers, grinding wheels, and flame cutters, as well as close-ups of crankshafts being lubricated.

While the strips and accompanying tapes were rolling, students were supposed to fill out special career-rating charts ("Your Interest Inventory"), marking down on a scale of 0 to 4 →

their level of desire to follow this particular career path. Their appetites for metalworking were to be further stimulated by tidbits from the instructor's cheat sheet: "Metalworking is one of the world's oldest trades. Working conditions can be hazardous when work is performed around metal and complex equipment, sometimes at great heights. The noise factor and working in a shop environment must also be considered. However, good wages and excellent benefits generally offset these conditions."

These strips are classic early 1970s, a delightful blend of two complementary aesthetics. There's the shop-teacher look of short-sleeve shirts, pocket protectors, blue aprons, horn-rims, Marine Corps tattoos, and Speidel watchbands. Then there's the grooviness of the fellas with mullet hairdos, Fu Manchu 'staches, muttonchops, and suede ankle boots. Despite the real-world locations, the photography in these strips is rich, beautiful, and strange. It makes you want to take up machining.

Well, maybe not. ■

MATH AND SCIENCE

MATH AND SCIENCE

Throughout the 1930s and 1940s, progressive education focused on making learning useful and a part of everyday life. Its critics stood at the schoolhouse door all the while. They complained that, compared with their peers in other nations, America's children just plain weren't being educated, a situation that was eroding our position in the world. Other nations had far higher standards and their youth were far more serious about learning, while ours were quaffing sodas at the malt shop with Archie and Veronica.

Major magazines ran derisive stories about school programs that seemed a joke, such as math classes in which students built cardboard bank branches and played at being bank presidents, tellers, and depositors waiting in line. Johnny can't make change, can't tell time, can't *read,* for Pete's sake.

As the 1950s and the cold war wore on, these criticisms became louder and shriller. Members of the defense establishment warned that America lacked decent scientists and engineers directly because of the inadequacy of public schools, and without them, America would lose the most important postwar competition: the space race.

Thirty-five years after we reached the moon, it's hard to remember the passion Americans felt for the space program. Except for rare disasters, NASA missions are pretty ho-hum these days, but in the late 1950s they were incredibly important.

To put it into perspective, think back to September 11, 2001, and how vulnerable we all felt, how worried about the future of the nation. That's the way many Americans felt after World War II. We had seen ideologues take over half the planet and creep right up to our shores. We had sacrificed lives and property and put progress on ice for nearly a decade. No one wanted to go through that again.

The witch hunt that was Senator Joe McCarthy and the House Committee on

SPUTNIK I

21

Sputnik, the first man-made satellite, changed American life, American politics, and American education. And it was only the size of a basketball. From *How Man Explores Space,* page 171

Un-American Activities was like nothing we've faced since. People were genuinely afraid that an alien force was subverting the government from inside, taking over Hollywood and using movies and TV, our favorite art forms, to subtly invade our minds with some evil agenda. It's hard now to understand how we could have let our own government disrupt and destroy so many lives, but at the time a great many people felt it was a price worth paying.

On October 4, 1957, the USSR successfully launched *Sputnik I,* the world's first artificial satellite. Weighing only 183 pounds, *Sputnik* passed right over our heads every hour and a half, carrying God knows what. Its four-ton space booster could be clearly seen with the naked eye as it hurtled overhead. Then the Soviets struck again: On November 3, *Sputnik II* was launched, captained by a female dog named Laika.

America freaked out.

This was a new kind of war. At a time when the world was divided between two powerful and competing ideologies, the Soviets were telling everyone on earth that they had progressed further and could take mankind farther than anyone else. Even more threatening, they were staking a claim in the sky, a newfound perch from which they could rain down bombs on anyone, anywhere. After the horrors of Hiroshima, people were quite willing to believe that technology and its masters were now capable of just about anything.

The future of America, of freedom, of the planet itself, seemed to be at stake. And this was not a war that would be won overnight. Not only did America's military and scientific communities need to tackle the problem immediately; future generations would have to be mobilized to continue holding the torch aloft.

The progressive agenda that had determined the course of education in this country seemed hopelessly inadequate. New emphasis had to be placed on math and science—real, pure, ➔

hard stuff that would stretch our kids' brains and prepare us to kick Red butt.

Of course, America wasn't losing the space race because kids didn't love trigonometry. While amping up math and science made us feel better and fostered the illusion that this was something we could all solve together if we really, really tried, our best hope was a former Nazi SS major.

The space program began in Nazi Germany under rocket pioneer Werner von Braun, working with the aid of slave labor from the Mittelbau-Dora concentration camp. The Nazis wanted von Braun to develop military missiles, but he and his team were always more interested in trying to get into orbit. When the first V2 rockets hit London during the blitz, von Braun muttered, "The rocket worked perfectly. It just landed on the wrong planet."

As the war ended and the Allies invaded Germany, von Braun and many other scientists fled south to surrender to the approaching American troops, rather than risk falling into the hands of the Soviets coming from the east. The Americans seized all the rockets and their components the Germans had abandoned, then shipped them stateside. Railroad cars carrying 140-foot V2 rockets and more than 100 German prisoner-of-war scientists arrived at Army bases on White Sands flats in New Mexico. The Americans had managed to snag the world's most advanced rocket scientists and their rockets in one fell swoop.

But in the early 1950s, Americans didn't seem that much more interested in space than the Germans had been. Though we had developed rockets that could soar 100 miles above the earth, our programs were primarily geared to designing new weapons. While we did conduct some experiments in the upper atmosphere, the armed forces' programs ultimately led to the development of intercontinental ballistic missiles and electronic guidance systems.

Then *Sputnik* streaked across the sky and the game changed.

Though it is strange and unpleasant on the moon, men will some day build shelter bases from which to explore.

American men, we hope. The outcome of the cold war seemed to hinge on who got to the moon first. From *Earth's Satellite, the Moon,* page 174

So how had the Soviets managed to beat von Braun and the Americans? The critical factor in the space race was internecine wrangling and territorialism among American government bureaucrats. Von Braun's group had been on the verge of launching the first U.S. satellite as far back as 1956. But President Eisenhower had decided that the navy's program (which was far less developed) would be the first to have a chance to launch it once it was ready. Rather than establish a scientifically coherent space program, the army, navy, and air force were squabbling and refusing to share data.

With the launch of *Sputnik,* a new course was quickly charted. In 1958 Eisenhower established a civilian space program, the National Aeronautics and Space Administration (NASA), which was given an extravagant ten-year, $100 million budget and a heady mission: to explore and occupy outer space.

This huge investment required major backing from the American people. All Americans had to feel that their support and participation were key to the nation's victory—and survival. In 1962 President Kennedy codified the mission ("... it will not be one man going to the moon ... it will be an entire nation. For all of us must work to put him there ..."), and by then America's students had been drilled over and again with that same message.

Making the moon seem exciting to schoolchildren was no mean feat. There weren't any 16-mm movies of the lunar surface, and words and diagrams in books weren't very vivid. So it fell to the humble filmstrip to become a powerful weapon in America's defense, putting the moon right inside our darkened classrooms and preparing us for the future, one frame at a time. ■

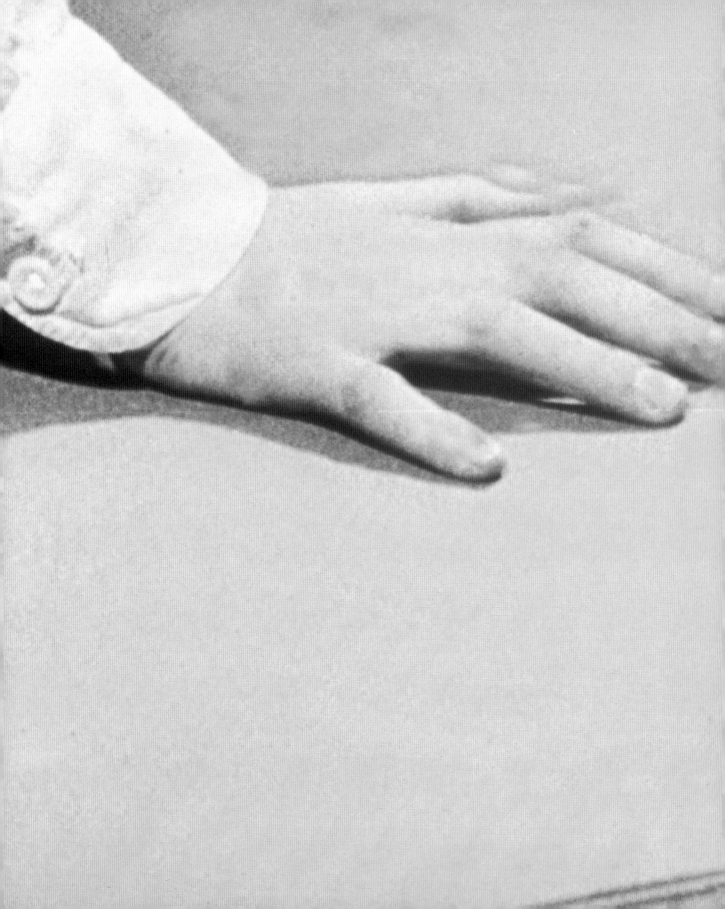

CHANGE IS GOOD

Making Change

Popular Science
Publishing Co., Inc., 1951

Jack's mom [1] sends him to buy bread and butter. At the store, [2] Mr. Brown, the grocer, impresses the simple boy by toting up a few figures without the help of a pencil, paper, or bar code scanner. Mr. Brown's store is different from your corner deli. His inventory is primarily cans, and, despite postwar inflation, bread is just 16¢ a loaf. [3] His point-of-sale marketing consists of a couple of hand-lettered signs. There are no Marlboro counter cards, no Budweiser change mat, no computerized cash register, and no lottery ticket come-ons.

Next, Jack hones his change-making skills in the class store. [4] Then, inspired by his scrape with capitalism, he decides to become a seed salesman and heads off to badger passersby with his wares.

Supermarkets did exist in 1951; the first ones appeared in the 1920s. But it wasn't till the rise of car culture and the suburbs that they really took off. In the early 1950s, the thin edge of the convenience food wedge appeared with the first Swanson frozen TV dinner: turkey with cornbread dressing, peas, and sweet potatoes. By 1955, most groceries were sold in supermarkets, and today very few children sell seeds in the street. [5] ∎

MAKING CHANGE

Jesse Osborn
Marguerite Gillaspy

"I need a loaf of bread and a pound of butter. Will you go to the store for me, Jack?" 6

"A dollar will be enough, I think. Butter is about 75 cents a pound, and bread is about 15 cents."

3

"88, 89, 90, 1 dollar." 14

2

"Mr. Brown, how do you make change without using pencil and paper to subtract?" 15

140 | "That is easy, Jack. Start with what the things cost. Add coins until you reach the amount that was given to you. Start by adding the smallest coins." 16

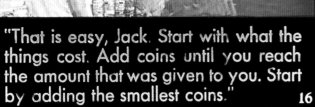

"64; 1 penny makes 65; 1 dime makes 75; 1 quaner makes the dollar." 20

"Mr. Brown showed me how he makes change at the store. May I be clerk to-day and show the other boys and girls?" 24

4

"Milk is 22 cents. You gave me three dimes or 30 cents. Here is your change 22, 23, 24, 25, 30." 28

(Jack thinks) That's an easy way to make change. Start with what the things cost. Add coins until you get up to the money given to you. **21**

"I am going to ask Mr. Dale if I may be clerk tomorrow in our school store." **23**

"I have $2." **31**

"Mr. Hill, I have 11 packages of vegetable seeds. You can plant them in your garden. They will cost you 55 cents." **39**

The children are offered the chance to sell garden seeds, and Jack approaches several of his neighbors.

What makes things float? Does floating depend upon the size of an object?

1

Take two objects the same size — a wooden block used for a buoy...

2

1

...and a brick used for an anchor.

3

2

The sponge weighs the same...

7

...as the lead sinker.

This model boat is so heavy that...

12

...when put in the water, it sinks...

13

The jar is so full that any water displaced by an object, will flow out into the glass.

25

The empty boat displaces water.

26

PHYSICS FOR FISHERMEN

Why Things Float

Key Productions/
Young America Films, 1953

Two boys head out on a lake armed with fishing tackle, sponges, bricks, beakers, and model boats. They aren't going to dump a body, they're going to learn some practical physics lessons. Through simple experiments that the viewers can reproduce later in class, the inquisitive pair discover how size, weight, and displacement affect flotation.

Like many filmstrips, this production was conceived as a 16-mm film on the same subject. The strip was either shot simultaneously or lifted from frames of the movie.

The styling of both kids is great: cuffed jeans, high-tops, saddle shoes, a Holden Caulfield–style deerstalker, [1] and a Gilligan cap, [2] all long before kids wore only T-shirts emblazoned with licensed characters and corporate logos. These boys are dressed typically for the period, yet they seem totally individual. They really look like a couple of kids goofing around (albeit with beakers and sponges). That may be a testament to the director's cinema verité or, more likely, to his meager budget. ∎

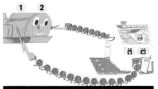

The generator pushes tiny bits of matter called electrons through the power wires. This movement of electrons is electric current. (6)

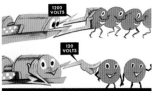

The strength of the push acting on electrons to get them to move is measured in volts. (7)

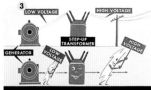

It is cheaper to send electricity at high voltage than at low voltage. A step-up transformer increases the voltage. (8)

To find the cost of electricity for one month, multiply the number of kilowatt-hours used in a month by the cost per kilowatt-hour. How much electricity did this family use? (11)

Six billion, billion electrons move through the filament of a one-hundred watt lamp every second it is on. (17)

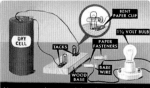

You can make a model outlet and plug. Slip the paper fasteners into the clips to complete the path for electrons. (18)

When a toaster is plugged in and turned on, the inside wires become red hot as electrons rush through them. (19)

The uncontrolled rush of electrons permitted by the short circuit could make the wall wires red hot and start a fire, if the fuse did not blow out. (27)

An overload of current, caused by using too many appliances at the same time, can also blow the fuse. (28)

WHERE DOES TOAST COME FROM?

Electricity at Home

David J. Goodman, Ph.D.,
for Charles Scribner's Sons, 1957

How does electricity work? The answers offered in this strip aren't hard-core physics; instead, abstract principles are presented with cute cartoons. Smiling balls represent electrons,[1] and hulking generators push them through wires.[2]

The filmstrip is eminently practical, explaining how to calculate your electric bill,[3] change a fuse, and make toast.[4] In 1957, the strip's author, Harry Milgrom, wasn't training future scientists (that would come in another year or two with the race to space). He was building an informed citizenry who were living with more and more electrical appliances as prosperity and technology advanced.

Milgrom continued to teach basic scientific principles to children for many years, writing fun books such as *Adventures with a Plastic Bag* and *Egg-ventures*. The producer of the strip was David J. Goodman, Ph.D., but like many filmstrips, it was distributed by a big textbook publisher, Charles Scribner's Sons. Let's toast them all. ∎

NATURE MAKES, WE TAKE

The Earth: A Great Storehouse

Eye Gate, 1950s

This strip, an overview of the natural resources the earth produces and the many ways in which we use them, conveys gratitude and wonder, a real appreciation of the earth's bounty.[1]

However, there is no mention of conservation; instead, we get the sense that the great storehouse is infinite and will continue to pour forth oil, coal, and iron as long as we need them. Despite the scarcities and rationing during the Depression and World War II, a new generation was being taught that we can consume as much as we choose and the bill won't ever come due.

Though Eye Gate was based in Queens, New York, this strip was shot in and around John Brown University, a small Christian college in rural Siloam Springs, Arkansas. The town was so small that the local concrete company's phone number had only three digits. [2] ■

FUNDAMENTALS OF SCIENCE
GRADES IV AND V

**THE EARTH—
A GREAT
STOREHOUSE**

TECHNICAL SUPERVISION-JOHN BROWN UNIVERSITY

COLOR PHOTOGRAPHY BY WILLIAM D. HOBBS

This is the earth on which we live.

There are many kinds of wildlife on the earth.

Such metals as iron, copper, aluminum, gold, and silver are found in the earth.

NATURAL RESOURCES

TREES

GREEN PLANTS

METALS

OIL

We call these materials natural resources.

Why does this house have glass windows?

McREYNOLDS CONCRETE
SILOAM SPRINGS = ARKANSAS
PHONE 470

Cement mixed with sand, gravel, and water makes a mixture called concrete.

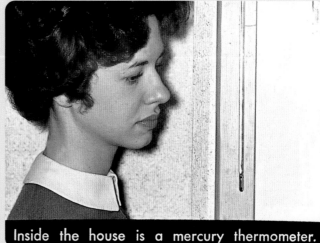

Inside the house is a mercury thermometer.

These articles are made of steel. How many other steel articles can you name?

Name some other things you have in your house that are made of copper.

Mercury is a liquid metal obtained from certain minerals in the earth.

Slate is a rock taken from the earth.

FOR USE AS A
MOTOR FUEL ONLY
CONTAINS
LEAD
(TETRAETHYL)

Lead ore comes from the earth. How is it used?

Tin comes from the earth. How is it used?

AIR—IT'S A GAS, MAN

Earth's Blanket of Air

Society for Visual Education, late 1950s

This beautiful strip was accompanied by recorded narration, probably on a 78-rpm record, which has disappeared and left the visuals mysterious and compelling. We'll never know what that girl has in the jar.[1] Is it blackberry jam? Mold?[2] Is that child measuring Kool-Aid?[3] What's the deal with the outline drawing of Alfred E. Neuman with all those arrows?[4] And what will that boy do with the condom he's inflating?[5]

The text on the mottled sponged backgrounds[6] and those gorgeous photos and diagrams (dig the room full of five hundred pounds of air[7]) seems to describe a series of experiments that prove that air exists, has weight, and exerts pressure.

I'm kind of glad the narration is lost. ∎

13

15

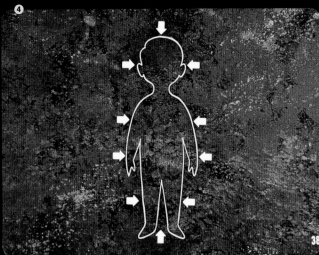

4

38

7

21

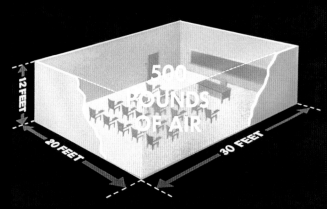

6

PROVING THAT
AIR TAKES UP
SPACE

RECORD BAND III

18

12 FEET

500
POUNDS
OF AIR

20 FEET

30 FEET

34

DON'T TAKE OUR PLANET FOR GRANTED

The Earth and Its Movements

Society for Visual Education, 1965

Why does Earth revolve? Why do we have seasons and night and day? What's our place in the Milky Way? During the half century before *The Earth and Its Movements* was produced, earth sciences had gradually disappeared from school curricula, and kids weren't being taught this elementary material. The progressive movement had put increasing emphasis on biology, which seemed to have more direct and useful impact on our daily lives—learning how a bean grows rather than the origins of the universe.

With the Soviets' launch of *Sputnik,* however, the political establishment became convinced that nuclear weapons and space exploration were to be the key markers of international military and economic status, so the National Science Foundation spent millions on a new curriculum. Whereas physical geography had virtually vanished from the classroom in 1950, by the mid-1960s, earth sciences, meteorology, oceanography, and space sciences were in with a vengeance.

Soon after the *Apollo* missions to the moon were completed, this emphasis quickly waned again, and despite this drop in attention, the earth continues to turn. ∎

8

10

27

28

ONE YEAR

600,000,000 MILES

49

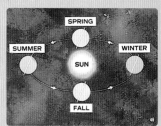

SPRING

SUMMER   WINTER

SUN

FALL

48

42

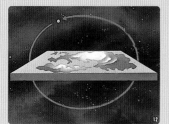

12

13

MILKY WAY

52

WHEN WILLARD SCOTT STILL HAD HAIR

Why Does It Rain, Snow, Hail, and Sleet?

Society for Visual Education, 1960

TV weathermen have always been fairly goofy, but this strip, chockablock with brand-new techno-developments, may give you a little respect for them. Here we learn about one of the first benefits of the space program: better weather reports, courtesy of satellites.

The images in this strip are a little schizo, flipping back and forth from Rocky and Bullwinkle–style cartoons [1] to tedious stock photos. [2] It's not enough to tell us that when a kettle boils it makes rain somewhere [3] or that we shouldn't swerve into telephone poles if it's glazing. [4] We need bleeding-edge snapshots of the earth from space and cutaway photos of the internal electronics of a TIROS (Television Infrared Observation Satellite). [5]

One of the advisers for the strip was Tetsuya Theodore "Ted" Fujita, the biggest name in severe storm research, a genius at the University of Chicago with an intuitive ability to figure out the mysterious workings of thunderstorms and tornadoes. "Mr. Tornado" was also the first person to create a color movie of the earth, knitting together dozens of satellite pictures to show the movements of clouds over the planet.

Can you say "mesometeorology"? ■

New WHY DOES IT RAIN, SNOW, HAIL AND SLEET?

Hail and sleet can be very unpleasant. What do you suppose causes them?

Water from this kettle is evaporating into the air. What is causing the evaporation?

The heat of the sun evaporates water from the surface of the earth.

The water vapor in the air differs from day to day and from place to place.

2

Do you think that snow can properly be called frozen rain? Explain.

100%   50%

Relative humidity is the amount of moisture in the air compared with the maximum amount which that air could hold at a given temperature.

FREEZING LEVEL

RAINDROPS BEGIN TO FREEZE HERE

Sometimes water droplets are carried by vertical air currents to a height where the temperature is below freezing. Here the droplets freeze.

Today, scientists are launching satellites designed to help weathermen learn more about weather.

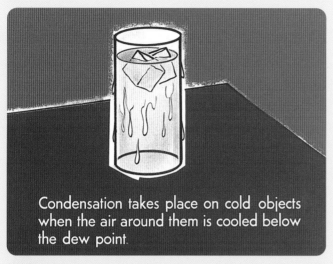

Condensation takes place on cold objects when the air around them is cooled below the dew point.

4

If the rain freezes upon touching the ground, trees, or other objects, it is called glaze.

What would happen to our world if there were no clouds?

5

This is TIROS (Television Infrared Observation Satellite). It serves weathermen by relaying information on cloud cover, temperature, and solar radiation.

MATH MADE EASY AS PIE

The Meaning of Fractions

Society for Visual Education, early 1950s

What's math for and why do we have to learn it? This strip has one answer: Mathematics isn't an art or a science, and it's not intended to expand one's mind and teach one to think abstractly. Numbers are purely practical; children are taught to recognize them and their sequences and to commit that information to memory. This strip is only a little less dry than reams of multiplication tables, and its function is the same—to drill numbers into kids' heads.

The applications for this kind of learning are eminently practical, too. By learning numbers from one to a hundred, you can make change for a dollar, share a pie, or dish out a casserole. You can be a grocer or a baker or a cafeteria worker. Math is useful in everyday life, and anyone can understand it. ➜

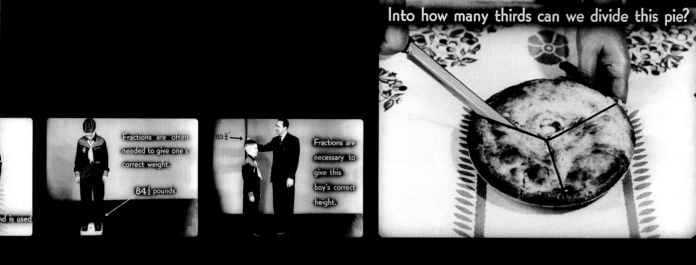

Into how many thirds can we divide this pie?

Fractions are often needed to give one's correct weight.

84½ pounds

...nd is used

53¾" Fractions are necessary to give this boy's correct height.

¼ DOLLAR   ½ DOLLAR

25   50

This dish has been divided into four equal

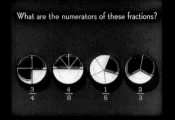
What are the numerators of these fractions?

$\frac{3}{4}$ $\frac{4}{8}$ $\frac{1}{5}$ $\frac{2}{3}$

Which is larger, $\frac{1}{2}$ of a pie or $\frac{1}{3}$ of a pie?

Sometimes we divide a whole into equal parts. Into how many equal parts has this brick of cheese been divided?

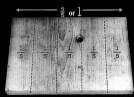
$\frac{5}{5}$ or 1

$\frac{1}{5}$ $\frac{1}{5}$ $\frac{1}{5}$ $\frac{1}{5}$ $\frac{1}{5}$

When the numerator and denominator of a fraction are equal, the fraction is always equal to one whole.

This is old math, the traditional approach that these pupils' teachers and parents learned when they were in elementary school. By the 1960s, it was scarcely good enough. The Soviets were trouncing our students with their knowledge of math and science. And—talk about practical applications—while we were learning to serve cake, they were learning to make lunar rockets. American kids had to be taught to think on their own and to be comfortable with the sorts of abstract concepts that were the gateway to working with physics and pure mathematics.

We didn't want any more grocers. We wanted rocket scientists. ∎

The numerator of a fraction is always written ABOVE the line.

Numerators

$\frac{1}{4}$ $\frac{2}{3}$ $\frac{4}{5}$

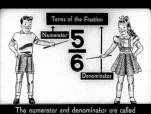
Terms of the Fraction

Numerator $\frac{5}{6}$ Denominator

The numerator and denominator are called the TERMS of the fraction.

Question 4: The _____ of a fraction tells us into how many equal parts the whole has been divided.

Question 7: If the denominator remains the same, the larger the numerator the _____ the fraction.

3. Why must the stickmen count of ten be changed? How will it be changed?

5. What count do the stickmen show? When one more sheep is counted, what change will be made?

A MEMORY MAN IS NEEDED

8. What will the new Counting Man do?

ONE HUNDRED

11. One Hundred is the new name for ten tens. Copy the number word. Copy the numeral.

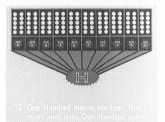

12. One Hundred means ten tens. How many ones does One Hundred name?

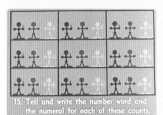

15. Tell and write the number word and the numeral for each of these counts. What will the next count be?

WHICH IS CORRECT?

16. Mary thinks: "The Tens Man is not needed." Bob thinks: "The set of Tens is empty."

22. One dollar will buy the same as how many dimes? As how many pennies?

WE SEE
$$\begin{array}{r} 75 \\ +25 \\ \hline \end{array}$$

WE THINK
$$\begin{array}{r} 70 + 5 \\ +20 + 5 \\ \hline 90 + 10 \end{array}$$

WE WRITE
$$\begin{array}{r} \overset{1}{75} \\ +25 \\ \hline 100 \end{array}$$

36. Write a placeholder equation for this addition and solve it.

ATTACK OF THE STICKMEN

Expanded Notation

Colonial Films, 1962

Around 1960, new math was introduced, to the consternation of most teachers and parents, who were completely clueless about this new approach. The old school way of learning math relied on drills and exercises, and on rewarding computation skills, speed, and accuracy. You just knew 6 × 8 was 48. You hadn't been taught the mathematic principles behind computation; the answer had been tattooed on your brain by rote. In the faculty lounge, teachers called it "grill and kill."

Overnight, boxes of colored wooden sticks called Cuisenaire rods and a focus on groups, set theory, and other abstract mathematical structures supplanted the old method. Math would become an intellectual exercise that would stretch the mind and a child's ability to reason. While standard arithmetic might help you function in the real world—help you saw a plank in three or make change at the gas station—new math was designed to create a generation of thinkers who could apply their analytical skills to improving the nation.

Kids would learn to take, say, a set of 6 and add it to a set of 3. The point was to see that 3 + 6 is the same as 6 + 3. Then, if they removed 1 set from the combined set, taking 3 from the group of 6 + 3 and getting 6, they would discover the *concept* of subtraction for themselves.

This sounds fairly straightforward, but when the lesson was in base 8 or base 6 (now don't make me stop and explain this) and threw in a lot of weird jargon, parents' heads started to spin. They couldn't help Johnny do his homework when it hinged on the sorts of assignments shown in this filmstrip: Tell a story problem. Write and solve a placeholder equation. What number is named by one finger of the Tens Man? ■

The moon is our nearest neighbor in the sky. It is much closer than the sun, and much, much closer than the other stars.

5 If the earth were hollow, it could hold nearly 50 moons.

Moon
Earth
The moon does not give off light like the sun and the stars do. It shines because it reflects light from the sun.

7 There's another reason why we will need safety suits. During the day, the temperature on the moon becomes hotter than boiling water (212 degrees Fahrenheit). Our suits protect us from the heat.

6

Face toward a person. Move around him in a circle. Keep facing him all the time.

1 Would you like to visit the moon to see what it is really like? Let's pretend we have a rocket ship which can carry us there. Here we go!

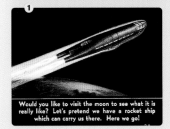
As we walk around, we feel very light and springy. We find that we can jump high in the air — or a long way forward — with very little effort.

2 3 We must also wear special safety suits to keep us from "blowing up." There is no air on the moon to press down on us. Without our safety suits, our veins and eardrums would burst.

8 4 Every now and then we notice tiny bullet-like particles striking the ground around us. They are meteorites. They would be very dangerous if we were not wearing our safety suits.

HELL IN SPACE

Our Neighbor, the Moon

The Jam Handy Organization, 1947

Well before the space race began, this virtual field trip made lunar travel seem possible but quite scary. We would travel to the moon in a rocket ship right out of Buck Rogers,[1] then descend to the surface in "safety suits"[2] so we wouldn't fry or blow up. (There's also a grisly warning that our veins and eardrums would burst without them.[3]) Everything would be deadly silent, and we would be surrounded by sharp, jagged mountains and huge craters[4] and bombarded with bulletlike meteorites. A caption tells us "This does not sound very pleasant, so we travel back to our rocket ship and take off for the earth." I'll say.

Despite the bleak picture, this strip has a friendly and chatty style. Oddly, even though after *Sputnik* travel to the moon went from a trip to hell to a patriotic duty and a grand adventure, space filmstrips became increasingly technical and dry.

This strip has some great images: the earth being ladled full of glowing moons;[5] boys walking in a circle to simulate the moon's orbit;[6] a boiling kettle mortised against jagged cliffs;[7] astronauts who look like Klansmen;[8] and paintings straight off a set for a TV serial like *Tom Corbett, Space Cadet.* ∎

We will be glad to get back to earth again. Our trip has made us more grateful for the fresh air, the water, the plants and animals of our earth.

WHY SPACE?
WHY NOW?

How Man
Explores Space

Society for Visual Education, 1965

In 1952, the International Council of Scientific
Unions decided that 1957–58 would be
International Geophysical Year. Not, perhaps,
the most thrilling cause for celebration. The ICSU also challenged the
world's scientists to launch the first satellites and map the earth's
surface. But before the United States could get its mechanical pencils
sharpened and its slide rules greased, the Soviets had fired *Sputnik* up into space. Then the Yanks
got scrambling. That very month, the Department of Defense had *Vanguard 1* on the launch pad.
Unfortunately, the first attempt exploded on the launchpad, and the next one veered off course
and disintegrated less than four miles from home. In January of 1958, they were more successful
with *Explorer 1*, which carried a cosmic ray detector that discovered the Van Allen magnetic
radiation belts that circle the earth. In the fall of 1958, Congress passed the Space Act, officially
creating NASA, and the U.S. began to pull into the lead of the space race.

Next up, *Pioneer 1* carried a magnetometer 71,700 miles from the earth to show how
complex the geomagnetic effects of the earth could be. Every few months, these first satellites →

HOW MAN
EXPLORES SPACE

From the Series
UNDERSTANDING
OUR EARTH
and UNIVERSE

ESCAPING EARTH'S GRAVITY

RECORD BAND I

GRAVITY

EARTH'S ROTATION

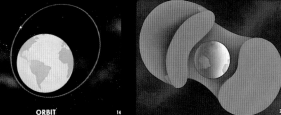

ORBIT

TIROS

were advancing human knowledge by leaps and bounds, proving that space wasn't some uninteresting void but a very complex region of magnetic fields and high-energy charged particles.

A practical application of all this new understanding came in April 1960 when TIROS-I ❶ showed how TV pictures could be used in a worldwide meteorological satellite information system. But after seventy-eight days, the first weather satellite tanked. In 1961, *Ranger* became the first U.S. effort to reach the moon. It wasn't until 1984 that a *Ranger* sent back data and pictures of the lunar surface. The first *Mariner* ❷ was launched to study Venus in 1962 and made the first ever measurements of the solar wind. Other *Mariners* went to Mars and Mercury.

For a kid watching this strip in 1965, America's mission to the moon was quickly becoming very real. ❸ Each of these accomplishments showed how it could be done and how the United Sates was going to do it. The images of space flight here seem so much more practicable and likely than the sci-fi filmstrips of a decade before. ■

All the space programs are catalogued, including *Sputnik I*, *Sputnik II*, *Explorer*, *Vanguard I*, *Pioneer*, *Discoverer*, and *Comsat*.

RANGER

A lesson in how man travels through space, dealing with antigravity boots, space food, life support, and the terrors of space debris.

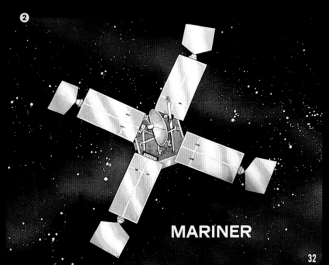

MARINER

32

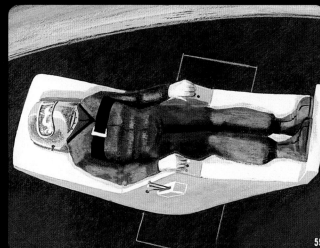

59

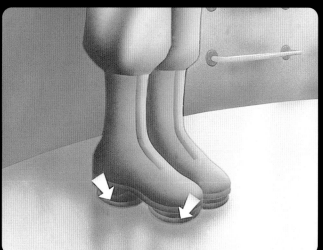

40

❸

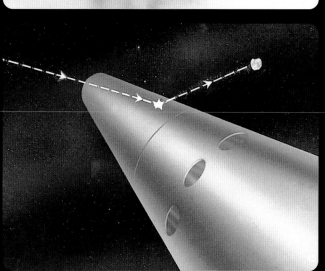

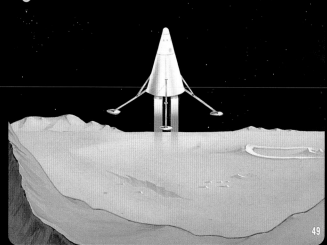

49

The moon shines mainly by reflected sunlight but we sometimes see part of it by reflected earthlight.

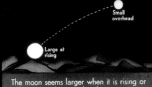

The moon seems larger when it is rising or setting than when overhead. Its apparent size on the horizon is an optical illusion.

Small overhead

Large at rising

(NOT TO SCALE)

AS SEEN FROM EARTH

NEW MOON

When the moon is between earth and sun, only the dark side faces us. The moon is invisible in the sunlight. It is NEW MOON.

1

AS SEEN FROM EARTH

GIBBOUS MOON WANING

VISIBLE FROM EARTH

The moon then wanes, rising after sunset, setting after sunrise. It is gibbous again but faces eastward.

Space is black with the sun, moon, earth, and stars shining brightly. There is no air, no sound, no weather or temperature, and no day or night.

In special space suits we step out on the airless moon. The weird scene is lighted by earth, shining in a black sky.

3

The mountains are sharp and jagged, for without air and water there is little erosion to wear them down. It is terribly hot by day and very cold at night.

2

Moon's gravity is only 1/6 that of earth. We weigh only 1/6 as much and are 6 times as strong. One step takes us about 15 feet.

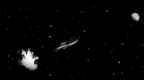

4

Though it is strange and unpleasant on the moon, men will some day build shelter bases from which to explore.

AN ECLIPSE OF THE SUN takes place when the moon passes in front of the sun and hides its light.

People sometimes imagine these markings look like a rabbit or a man on the moon.

SEA OF COLD
SEA OF SHOWERS
SEA OF SERENITY
SEA OF CRISIS
OCEAN OF STORMS
COPERNICUS
SEA OF VAPORS
SEA OF TRANQUILITY
KEPLER
SEA OF CLOUDS
SEA OF FECUNDITY
TYCHO

Actually the dark patches are lowlands and the light patches are highlands with mountains and craters.

We see only one side of the moon since it rotates on its axis only once a month (X always faces the earth).

ROTATION

What does the telescope show?

The crescent moon. Note the features visible along the terminator (the boundary between the light and dark sides).

The gibbous moon. Note how craters and mountains are best seen on the terminator where the rising sun casts shadows.

The full moon. The sun shines directly down on the moon. There are no shadows and fine details disappear.

There are many jagged mountain ranges on the moon. Here we see the Apennines, some of which rise 20,000 ft. above the plains.

What is it like on the moon?

What would we see if we went there?

5

OCCULTATION

As the moon moves eastward in its orbit, it sometimes passes in front of stars or planets. This is called OCCULTATION.

MOON PULLS

THE CREST

The pull of the moon's gravity raises the water in the ocean several feet. It also pulls the earth's crust up several inches.

SO, IS IT MADE OF CHEESE?

Earth's Satellite, the Moon

Society for Visual Education, 1960

How do we get kids all fired up about going to the moon? Why, let's force-feed them black-and-white charts and tons of new vocabulary they'll never use again! And so the strip begins: perigees and apogees and the waning and waxing of the gibbous moon. . . .❶

Just as the class is nodding off after two dozen frames of tedium, we shift gears to a travel brochure for the future. "A rocket ship could reach the moon in about nine and one half hours at seven miles per second. . . . Many scientists feel this will be possible before the year 2000." Now we see cool Captain Video images as astronauts in welding helmets cavort across the lunar tundra.❷ "In special space suits we step out on the airless moon. The weird scene is lighted by the earth, shining in a black sky." We're told about the inhospitable atmosphere, "dry and dead," studded with volcanoes and meteors and jagged mountains.❸ "Though it is strange and unpleasant on the moon, men will someday build shelter bases from which to explore."❹ Sounds great—let's go!

But after a few spectacular lunar photos from Lick Observatory, the fun is over and we're back to occultation,❺ penumbra, neap tide. . . . ■

THE END OF THE MOON

THE MOON TURNS RED

The Moon–Our Nearest Neighbor in Space

Eye Gate, ca. 1960

This filmstrip opens with three recent and—in the context of the cold war space race—daunting developments as unmanned Soviet spacecraft land on the moon and the Russkies began claiming its landmarks. There's the Moscow Sea, Tsiolkovsky Crater, and the Soviet Mountains.❶ What's next ... Neil Armstrongovich?

It's unusual to have a strip that presents such fresh information. Most were designed to have a long shelf life, but the pitch of space fever meant that new strips with late-breaking details were being rushed to schools in this period. Time was running out for the U.S.A.

Time and again, this lesson reaffirms the moon's proximity to the earth (it's right there!)❷ with out-of-scale diagrams that make it seem that any geriatric could lob a Whiffle ball into a lunar crater.❸ It claims that reaching the moon has been man's dream for centuries and implies that most scientific discoveries have been steps on the ladder toward the moon.

The final frames are fantasy projections of space ships with U.S.A. emblazoned on their flanks, wistfully wondering, "Will they find living things on other planets?"❹ ■

FUNDAMENTALS OF SCIENCE
GRADES IV AND V
THE MOON–
OUR NEAREST
NEIGHBOR IN SPACE
TECHNICAL SUPERVISION–JOHN BROWN UNIVERSITY
COLOR PHOTOGRAPHY BY WILLIAM D. HOBBS

On September 12, 1959, a Soviet-launched rocket reached the moon.

On October 4, 1959, the Soviet Union launched a rocket designed to go around the moon.

①

On October 27, 1959, the Soviet Union released the first picture of the hidden side of the moon.

All through history, man has dreamed of reaching the moon or some other heavenly body.

John Kepler formulated laws for the motion of heavenly bodies, and Isaac Newton discovered the law of gravitation.

②

Based on these laws, the path of a moon missile is calculated today.

178 This law made it possible to calculate the velocity needed for a missile to escape the earth's pull.

Let us look at the moon.

A week later, the full moon appears.

More on the timing of the phases of the moon and why it gets eclipsed.

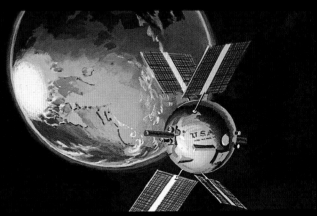

Today, we have man-made moons that travel around the earth.

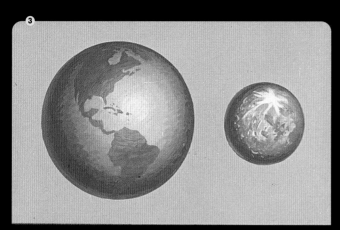

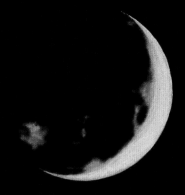

The moon is a round ball like the earth, only smaller.

Shortly after new moon, we see a thin crescent moon-the first crescent.

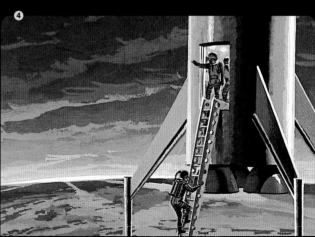

Some day we may have man-made moons or rockets that will carry people into space.

Will they find living things on other planets?

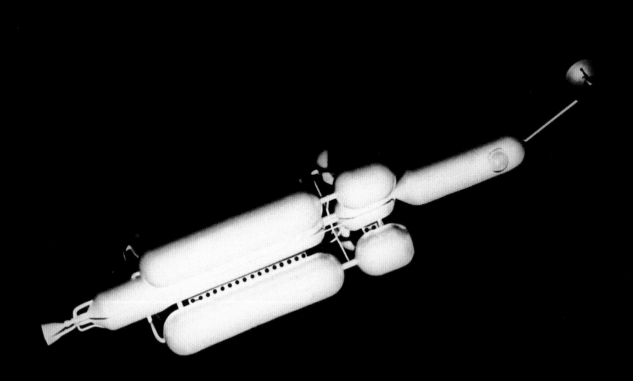

The manned moon ship may look like this.

Telescopes are kept in buildings called OBSERVATORIES. This shows Mt. Palomar Observatory in California.

This is a large refractor at Lick Observatory in California. Its lens is 36 inches in diameter.

This is the world's largest reflecting telescope at Mt. Palomar, California. Its mirror is 200 inches in diameter.

Here we see an astronomer at work with the 200-inch telescope.

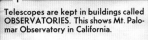

Astronomers find what stars are made of and what they are like from this instrument called the SPECTROGRAPH.

Most modern astronomy work is done with cameras. This Schmidt telescope is used to photograph the heavens.

The rocket reaction engine is the only type now known which can operate in space

A manned space station may be the depot for a trip to the moon.

BEAM ME TO THE MOON

Work of Astronomers and Space Travel

Society for Visual Education, ca. 1958

Undated (like most Society for Visual Education strips), this strip was created sometime between the launch of *Vanguard I* in early 1958 and the Soviet lunar missiles in the fall of 1959 (though *Sputnik*, probably already ingrained in every schoolchild's head, is conspicuously absent). It joined the wealth of new filmstrips about the space program that were rushed to schools at the time.

Work of Astronomers and Space Travel includes some beautiful images of the inside of the observatory on Mount Palomar ❶ and some great science fiction illustrations, including a Jules Verne rocket of the year 2000, ❷ a space station design that is straight out of *2001: A Space Odyssey,* ❸ and a moon ship that looks like one of those balloon sculptures that clowns make at kids' birthday parties. ❹ These fantastic illustrations are a foreshadowing of how much astonishing progress would occur in space technology over the next eleven years. ∎

High speeds with new kinds of power in the future may open the way to the distant places in space.

1

An aviator radioed he had seen a flying saucer disappear in the clouds. He saw no signs of life on it.

Some years ago, Orson Welles caused a near panic by broadcasting a report of an invasion of the earth by Martians.

In our enjoyment of life on this earth, how many of us ask whether there is any life elsewhere in the universe?

Years ago, scientists speculated on the existence of life on the sun. We know, today, that it is impossible.

Venus is a mystery planet. It has been pictured as a tropical swamp.

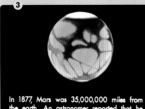

3

In 1877, Mars was 35,000,000 miles from the earth. An astronomer reported that he had seen canals on the planet.

2

The frozen atmosphere of Jupiter is 6000 miles deep and exerts a pressure of 5000 tons to the square inch.

Between Mars and Jupiter there is a belt of asteroids that circle around the sun in their orbits. No life exists on them.

Saturn has nine moons. Titan, the largest of the moons, is unfit for life because of its poisonous atmosphere.

JEEPERS, ALIENS!

Life on Other Planets

Eye Gate, probably mid-1950s

What's really exciting about space? What do we *really* want to know about? Aliens! It was in the fifties that they seemed the most real. In 1947, while Americans were fretting that the Reds were infiltrating our government and the movie industry, the first flying disks were spotted in Washington State [1] and the Air Force was denying that aliens were being held at Roswell. In 1950, *True Magazine* introduced the idea that those UFOs were actually alien spacecraft and that the government was withholding evidence about them. Whom could we trust? Was it a conspiracy? Throughout the late 1950s, there were further claims of alien sightings and contacts, and the government went back and forth, investigating and denying.

Conspiracy theorists will view this filmstrip as a bit of a wet blanket. It claims that though people have speculated about UFOs for ages, it's highly unlikely that there's life on any nearby planets. The sun's far too hot, Jupiter's too cold, [2] Venus has no oxygen, Saturn's full of marsh gas, and the Martian canals [3] are just a bunch of volcanic cracks. Oh, well—unless it's another sinister government plot to throw us off track with logic and fact. ∎

Astronomers believe that there are other solar systems like ours, but they are too far away for them to see signs of life.

PROPAGANDA

PROPAGANDA

Marketers and industry groups, eager to develop connections that can turn into lifelong buying habits, have always been interested in reaching children. Even if their products are sold only to adults, they can't resist the chance to talk to future consumers while they're still malleable. Who knows how they may influence Dad as he takes his car for an oil change or Mom as she walks down the grocery store aisle?

Check out school cafeterias and you'll find Taco Bell and Arby's subcontracted to provide lunches. Channel One, a news network created specifically for schools, brings commercials right into 40 percent of American classrooms. In science class, you'll find logos for Dow, DuPont, Exxon, and other corporations on the materials they've provided the teacher. Their materials encourage teachers to become propagandists, and schoolkids will always associate their lessons with these giant companies. Worse still, their agendas and biases color the information they provide.

Schools have long been facilitators of this dialogue between big companies and small children. They're quite happy to ease their limited budgets with the discounted or free educational materials that production companies, publishers, and marketers willingly provide. They generally leave whether or not the materials actually get into the classroom to the teacher's discretion, but if the presentation is well done and useful and the sponsor stays reasonably in the background, those materials often become part of the curriculum.

Nonetheless, watching a filmstrip built to fit some corporate agenda was like listening to Dad talk about the office. You vaguely understood the topic and recognized some of the characters, but you were utterly bored because, despite the speaker's passion, it had little to do with you. The logos, however, were stickier. For a minimal investment in what they probably told themselves was public service, big corporations could make impressions on young consumers that would last a lifetime. ■

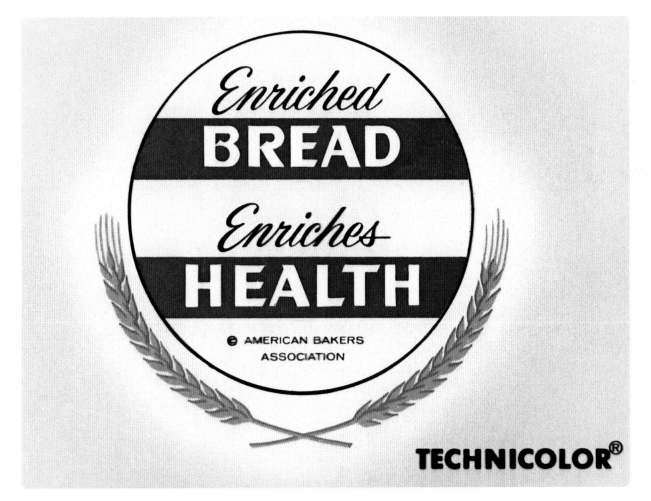

If this feels more like an advertising slogan
than a school lesson, that's because it is.
From *Your Daily Bread*, page 189

As you watch this film, you will learn how your daily bread is baked, and why it is so good for you.

CHEMICALS MAKE BREAD YUMMY

Your Daily Bread

The American Bakers' Association,
early 1960s

Our lesson begins with a historical retrospective of primitive people baking bread on stones and bricks.❶ Even the Colonists❷ made bread pretty much the way it was made several thousand years before. But progress has finally arrived, and now bread is made in gleaming factories.❸ Unmanned machines—a far cry from the half-naked, brown-skinned people we saw in the first few frames—crank out loaf after perfect loaf.

Those machines are great, but the American Bakers' Association wanted us to know that the true hallmark of our evolution was in modern bread's list of ingredients. In addition to mere flour, yeast, and salt, we were using "enrichment wafers"❹ to make modern food for modern folks. Now, who wouldn't want to be "enriched"?

Over the past one hundred years, certain additives made a major impact on diseases. In the 1920s, salt was iodinated to eliminate goiter. Ten years later, our milk was supplemented with vitamin D. Nowadays, we consume calcium in orange juice and iron filings in cereal to build stronger bones. Our supermarkets are full of nutriceuticals. ➜

YOUR DAILY BREAD

Long ago people hunted wild animals for food.

❶

The first bread was baked on heated stone and was like a thin, hard pancake.

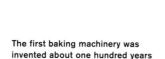

The first baking machinery was invented about one hundred years ago.

stones
ake.

The Greeks and Romans invented the first real ovens.

Early bakers in America used tools and methods much like those used by the ancient Romans and Greeks.

Here is a modern bakery.

The idea of fortifying bread had been around for quite some time, but most consumers and manufacturers felt little incentive to spend money for the chemicals. However, during World War II, the U.S. and British governments decided to boost their nations' health by fortifying manufactured foods. Propaganda campaigns and large government contracts pushed the new products into every pantry. By 1943, all bread bought by the U.S. Army contained additives, specifically three B vitamins (niacin, riboflavin, thiamin)❺ and iron. The scientific reasoning behind this selection is still disputed, and many nutritionists contend that convincing people to eat whole wheat bread would probably have done far more to improve our health.

After the war, communications like this filmstrip helped to make sure Americans continued to equate ingesting chemical vitamins with living "a happier, healthier life."❻ ■

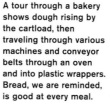

A tour through a bakery shows dough rising by the cartload, then traveling through various machines and conveyor belts through an oven and into plastic wrappers. Bread, we are reminded, is good at every meal.

Enrichment Wafers Supply – Iron – Niacin – Riboflavin – Thiamin.

The ingredient room is the bakery's pantry.

Bread's Ingredients.

SHORTENING

YEAST

SALT

DRY MILK

SUGAR

FLOUR

ENRICHMENT WAFERS

Your daily bread is one of the foods that helps you lead a happier, healthier life.

TOMMY GETS TO RIDE THE "LIFELINE OF THE NATION"

Tommy Takes a Train Trip [1]

Railroads and National Defense [2]

Railroads and Clothing [3]

Railroads and Our Mail [4]

Railroads and the Food We Eat [5]

Dudley Pictures Corporation, early 1950s

Tommy has the time of his life riding in a Pullman, supping on pie and ice cream, [6] then retiring to his roomette and summoning his porter [7] to make up his bed. Meanwhile, on other trains, dishes, bags of cement, button cards, love letters, and hogs are being rushed from coast to coast, making our nation great.

Why did schoolchildren need filmstrips celebrating the role of the railroad in our everyday lives? And why the ridiculous hyperbole of the railroad taking credit for everything of value in America? Ask the sponsor, the Association of American Railroads, one of Washington's oldest lobbying groups. It was determined to get its industry back on track and to convince the passengers and freight shippers of tomorrow that the country couldn't function without the train. ➜

Tommy is going to travel all by himself to visit his grandparents.

His father takes him to the station.

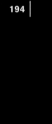
ion.

They go to the platform as the train pulls in.

He waves to his father from the window.

The train conductor collects Tommy's train ticket . . .

He goes to the dining car for dinner.

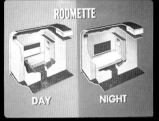
ROOMETTE
DAY NIGHT

When the time comes, Tommy gets ready for bed.

He presses a button to call the porter.

The conductor signals "All aboard."

He orders a good dinner with pie and ice cream.

After dinner Tommy walks back through the train.

Sleeping cars have several types of accommodations.

The bed is already made.

Next morning he repacks his suitcase.

The train pulls into his station and Tommy gets off.

His grandfather meets him.

Of course, trains do matter to America, but not the way they used to when the board of the AAR was in its prime. At the beginning of the twentieth century, railroads were king, and their owners were enormously wealthy. With the Great Depression, however, they slipped into red ink and came under government bankruptcy protection—much like today's airlines.

During World War II, the railroads, reinvigorated by the defense effort, entered their busiest period ever. Troops were routinely moved around the country by rail, and because of gas and tire rationing, many civilians had to travel by train instead of by car.

But the momentum didn't last. Many years of government regulation created a calcified, overregulated industry. An excise tax, added to ticket prices to discourage civilians from filling up train seats during the war, remained in partial effect until the 1960s, further dampening trains' ability to compete. Government subsidies no longer propped up the rail business but went to build new roads and airports. Those improvements meant trucks, buses, cars, and planes could haul away the freight and passenger business. Competing independent railroad companies undercut each other, and their management continued to behave like a monopoly, dictating rules and conditions to their freight customers and passengers. Truckers, far more customer-responsive, became the carrier of choice.

The rail industry puttered along, refusing to read the writing on the wall. By the 1970s, airlines had been deregulated and picked up the vast majority of passenger travel while the railroads carried less than 10 percent. Soon all those passenger train companies vanished into government-owned Amtrak and, today, only freight trains remain a meaningful part of our transportation chain. ∎

RAILROADS AND NATIONAL DEFENSE

Produced by DUDLEY PICTURES CORPORATION

When danger threatens, America prepares for defense.

The nation's defense calls for a tremendous job of transportation.

It is the sort of transport job that can be done only by railroads.

Trains move millions of tons of materials.

For example, trains carry the iron and steel . . .

. . . to make weapons, munitions and other equipment.

Trains transport fighting men to camps, naval stations, and embarkation points.

Since World War II, they have spent more than five billion dollars on improvements . . .

. . . adding thousands of new locomotives . . .

So, in peace or war, railroads provide our nation's basic transportation service.

They are truly **The Lifeline** of the Nation.

③

RAILROADS AND THE CLOTHES WE WEAR

Produced by DUDLEY PICTURES CORPORATION

America's **No. 1** Car

The most important car in America is the railroad freight car.

It transports almost everything we use in our daily lives.

Clothing for instance . . .

Railroads carry bales of cotton to the mills, where it is made into cloth.

Railroads haul leather for shoes . . .

. . . rayon and nylon and the materials of which they are made . . .

. . . materials for buttons . . .

Much clothing moves in overnight

. . . and next morning brought to stores

As raw materials and finished goods,

RAILROADS AND OUR MAIL

PRODUCED BY Dudley Pictures Corporation

Have you ever stopped to think how much mail is carried by train?

You drop your letters, properly addressed and stamped, into the mail box...

...and a mail truck picks them up and takes them to the post office...

Then the mail is trucked to the railroad station...

...and loaded into mail cars known as Railway Post Offices -- post offices on wheels.

UNITED STATES MAIL
RAILWAY POST OFFICE

While the train speeds along, clerks sort the mail.

And so, transported by train, your mail reaches its destination...

...and is delivered to the door.

Most of your parcel post packages come to you by railroad...

...and at Christmas time railroads carry almost all your holiday mail.

Day and night, storm or fair weather, railroads transport the mail the year around.

RAILROADS AND THE FOOD WE EAT

PRODUCED BY Dudley Pictures Corporation

We are a well fed people.

...and our country is one of the greatest food producing nations in the world.

The dairy industry supplies us with milk, cream, butter and cheese.

From plowing the fields to marketing the crops, railroads play a vital part.

Railroads carry farm implements to the farmer.

Railroads carry beef cattle from the western ranges to packing plants.

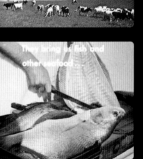

They bring us fish and other seafood...

Railroads carry grains from elevators to mills...

...to be made into flour for bread, pies, and cakes.

Good food builds healthy bodies.

We enjoy more and better food because of our railroads.

We use cotton chiefly for clothing... 2

...and for industrial products.

All cotton was once picked by hand... 8

...but now, modern picking machines are used in many areas.

But it takes the work of many people and many machines to make this cotton <u>boll</u> into useful products.

6

They are then fed into the <u>carding machine</u>, which cleans and removes the short fibers, and brings the long fibers together. 21

...such as these plastic steering wheels. 16

Sometimes, colorful patterns are printed on the cloth. 38

Cotton serves us in our homes. 40

THE COTTON-PICKING FACTS

How We Get Our Cotton

The Textile Information Service, 1950

This is another strip celebrating a boring industry most kids probably took for granted. With images of gleaming steering wheels floating in the air [1] and bolts of leopardskin or floral fabric, [2] the Textile Information Service tried to pull cotton off the plantation and make it modern. Sadly, images of carding machines, [3] spinning mills, and African Americans picking cotton [4] did more to remind the viewer of the Old South. Still, why was the industry bothering?

In 1950, King Cotton was beginning to feel the first threat to its monopoly. Synthetics had become important strategic initiatives during World War II; with no access to Japanese silk, the U.S. government had to find a new source for parachutes and tents, so DuPont had directed all its efforts to speeding up the development of nylon, the miracle fiber. Soon acrylic and polyester were also taking the market by storm.

With peace came new opportunities—women with money to spend loved the new textiles. They could be cleaned at home, didn't need much pressing, and outlasted cotton. The housing boom also led to great demand for nylon carpeting. In the new America, where looking sharp, crisp, and neat were signs of success, synthetics were a hit.

But wait! Cotton, we learn from this strip, is incredibly useful and can be turned into Band-Aids, cooking oil, and tires. Whatever. Fifty years later, the Cotton Council is still trying to sell us on "the fabric of our lives." Wisely, it's using fashion and comfort rather than images of automatic spoolers and conveyor belts to get into our closets. And it's staying out of our classrooms. ■

STRETCHING THE TRUTH ABOUT RUBBER

How We Get Our Rubber

Young America Films, 1958

Rubber, how fascinating! It can be as soft as a cushion or hard as a bowling ball. Do go on. Don't worry, this strip does go on (and on), as latex is milked out of trees, then spun, strained, and solidified. We see brown-skinned people[1] pouring, scraping, and rolling, then cutting, drying, compressing, and wrapping.

But that's not all—there's also *synthetic* rubber! Here it is, looking like some sort of giant tongue,[2] and twenty miraculous steps later . . . a bunch of rubber gloves![3] Let's look at more black-and-white photos of it being rolled, extruded, mixed, and vulcanized. And suddenly it's a mattress![4]

Regardless of all this tedium, rubber had been a critical part of the war effort. When the Japanese took over much of the Far East, they also shut down access to the rubber plantations. It became so scarce that gasoline was rationed so people wouldn't wear down their tires. Government land was turned over to grow *Parthenium argentatum*, a rubber-producing plant. →

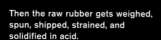
Then the raw rubber gets weighed, spun, shipped, strained, and solidified in acid.

... and wrapped for shipment.

A milky, white fluid, latex, oozes out of the cut and is caught in a cup.

begin made

The solid raw rubber is then rolled into sheets.

Scientists had been working on a practicable synthetic alternative since the turn of the century, but during the war, government-sponsored research began in earnest. More money was spent on this problem than on developing the atomic bomb. Even after access to Asian sources was restored, synthetic rubber remained popular, and since 1960 it has dominated the industry.

U.S. Rubber, the sponsor of this strip, has always been committed to promoting itself to kids. In the 1940s, it footed all the bills for the Little League World Series, and it is still active in youth soccer leagues. In the 1960s, the company changed its name to Uniroyal, developed a cute tiger mascot with windshield eyes, and built an eight-story tire for the World's Fair, which still stands in Detroit.

Despite the exhaustive nature of the strip, it omits one of the applications that would probably be most relevant to schoolchildren: The U.S. Rubber Company was the inventor and world's largest manufacturer of sneakers. They made the Keds almost all kids were wearing at the time. ∎

... and poured into a mold which looks like a large waffle iron.

The story of this man-made rubber begins at the synthetic rubber plant.

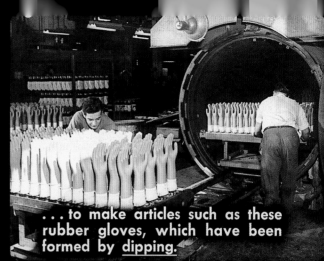

...to make articles such as these rubber gloves, which have been formed by dipping.

4

And we sleep on rubber. Whatever its use, rubber serves us well.

YOUR BACK WHEEL'S GOING FORWARD

How to Ride Your Bicycle Safely

Audio Visual School Service for Mobil Oil, mid-1950s

In a long and painful analogy, Captain Sam teaches Mary and Bob [1] how to ride their bikes safely by taking them through all the maintenance required to keep an airplane flying. [2] It's a long way around the block, though it never occurs to anyone to put on a helmet.

Sam warns them against doing all the things that make biking fun: hitching, [3] hot-dogging, and carrying groceries. The strip concludes with unlikely hip-to-be-square results: The kids are so fired up by the cap'n's lessons that they use a filmstrip projector [4] to create a giant mural, which has their whole peer group scrambling to become incredibly safe riders, too.

This stylish filmstrip features some great design and illustration, particularly of the block-long, sinuous cars, [5] and the cyclists look like dorks next to these sleek monsters. Ultimately, of course, Mobil [6] didn't sponsor this strip just to promote chain oiling and saddle adjusting, but to embed the image of the helpful, bow-tied Mobil mechanic squarely in the soft, impressionable minds of young America. ■

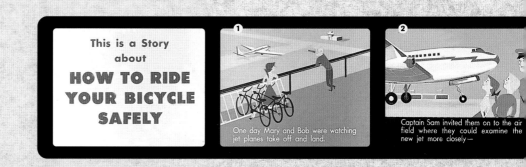

This is a Story about **HOW TO RIDE YOUR BICYCLE SAFELY**

One day Mary and Bob were watching jet planes take off and land.

Captain Sam invited them on to the air field where they could examine the new jet more closely—

e air
the

Bob asked, "What does it take to learn to be an expert pilot?"

Captain Sam joined Mary and Bob on his bike as they headed towards the town.

Bob and Mary rode past a red light as the Captain waited for the light to change.

That red light is meant for us as much as it is meant for autos. Let me show you a few bicycle safety rules.

Now, said Captain Sam, there are a few "don'ts" in bicycle riding which I will describe rather than demonstrate.

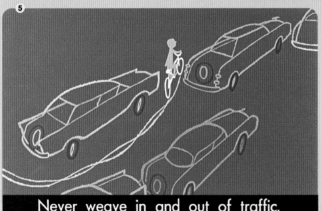

5

Never weave in and out of traffic, because the auto driver cannot see you coming.

In general, keep your bike clean and in tip-top shape. It will last longer and ride safer.

3

Never hitch on other vehicles, or try stunts.

6

As they passed the service station, Mary noticed her father having his car checked.

4

With the aid of a filmstrip projector they made a huge mural.

They planned it so that it told the story of bicycle safety as they understood it.

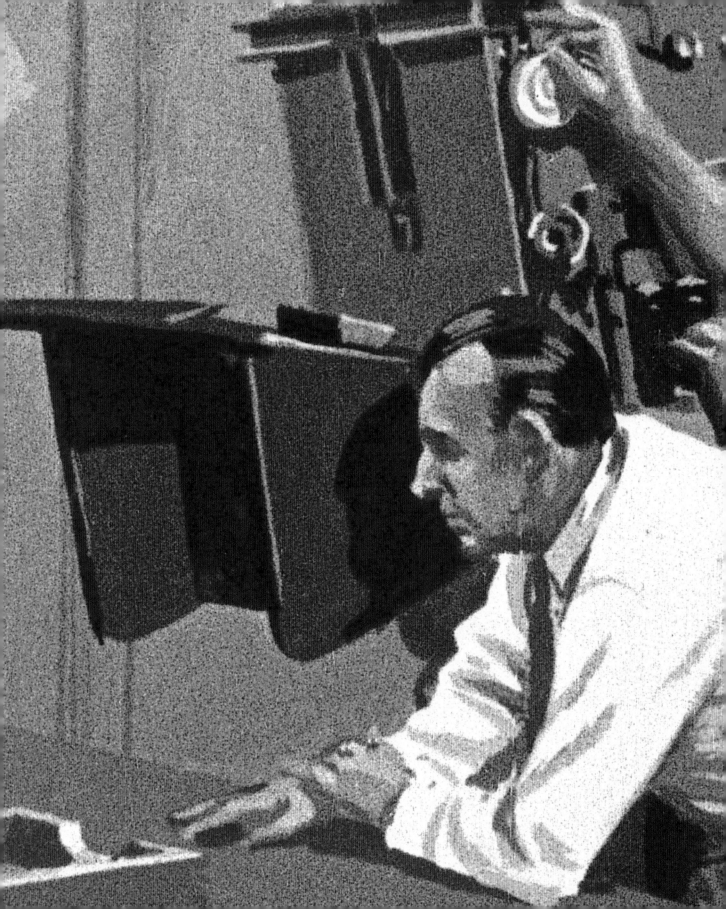

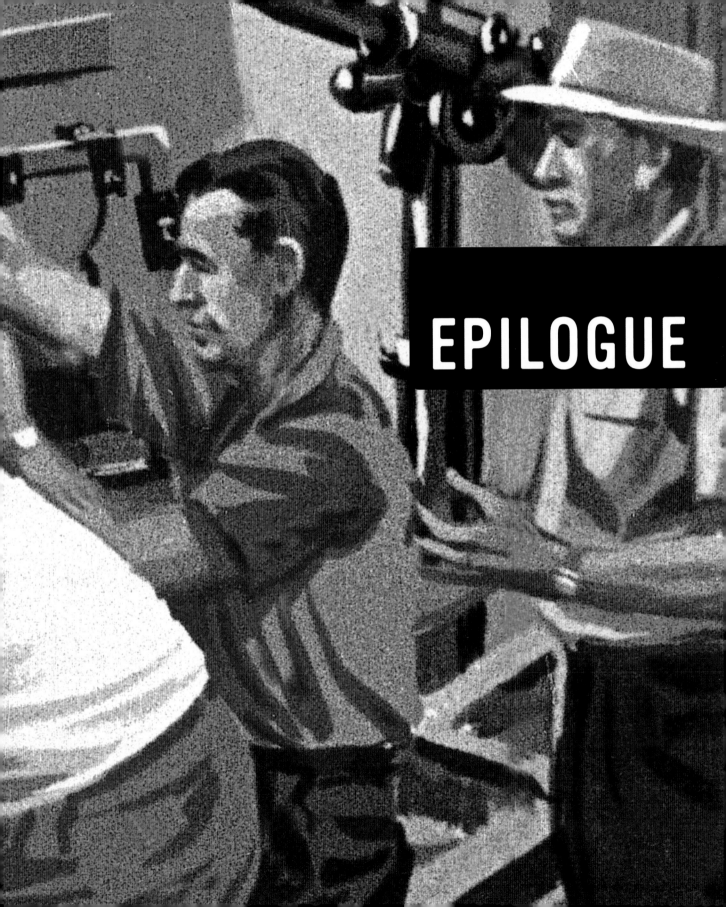

EPILOGUE

WHAT EVER HAPPENED TO FILMSTRIPS?

Filmstrips had their heyday in the 1940s and 1950s, when they were considered modern and efficient. By the early 1960s, they were becoming associated with a view of education that was controlling and formulaic.

After the conservative clampdown on progressive ideals that came in the late 1950s, the pendulum took another swing. The late 1960s and early 1970s were a new period of experimentation, and the "free school" movement swept the nation. Growing out of the radical social criticism of the period, it rejected anything that smacked of control and tradition—grades, honors, competition, tests, textbooks, and lesson plans, even the very idea that an absolute body of knowledge existed, that there were things that children should learn at all. The only thing that students were to be taught was the importance of self-expression and individual liberty. Theoretically, they were left to decide for themselves what they would do, and what they would learn and from whom. This was progressivism in the extreme.

The most radical critics called for the abolition of schools altogether, claiming that they were nothing but prisons that brainwashed social values into their young victims and continued to exist only because of long-term collusion between educators and government functionaries looking to preserve their jobs. Obviously, the idea of sitting in the dark watching a prefab lesson in a filmstrip was as dead as Brylcreem.

The free school movement was short-lived, collapsing under the very chaos it encouraged. Kids ran wild, parents complained. Something had to be done. More regimentation returned to schools by the early 1970s (but too late for the filmstrip). Filmstrips were phased out, not just because they were square (or rectangular, to be precise). They were ultimately replaced in the classroom by two new and robust technologies: the VCR and the PC.

It turns out, however, that old filmstrips never die, they simply fade away (although the

Schools use motion pictures as a means of communication.

From *Modern Means of Communications*, produced by Eye Gate.

three dyes that make up color film fade at different rates, tending to leave the strips looking magenta). School budgets have always been limited, and durable educational materials can have a long half-life, even if they are well past their prime and utility. In underfunded school libraries across the country, you can still come across drawers full of neat rows of filmstrip canisters. They're rarely checked out anymore; their celluloid is growing brittle and milky, and eventually, like a long-forgotten lesson, they'll disappear altogether.

Yet we can learn a lot from the past. When we look back at these lessons, we see mistakes—mistakes that look funny to us today. We see naïveté, provincialism, and crudeness, timidity, paternalism, sexism, and racism. So many of these filmstrips were created without great care, attention, or the supervision of an education professional. Like poorly made shoes, they had the ability to mold and distort our progress when our bones and minds were still growing.

But there are also many positive things in these strips: community, wisdom, decency, order, and a total lack of irony and cynicism. It would be a shame if these values were to fade away along with the dyes on our aging filmstrips. ■

A DAY ON THE FARM

I was just nine. I had recently arrived in Pakistan to live with my grandparents, who had enrolled me in the Lahore American School. Our classroom was surrounded by paddocks filled with bony bullocks, and vultures sometimes stole our sandwiches off the lunch tables, but the school's curriculum and culture were straight out of the Midwestern United States. I had been raised in England and Australia. I knew nothing about America except what I had read about in books and seen on the *Mickey Mouse Club*. Within days, I learned the words to "Shenandoah" and "My Darling Clementine." I was on my way.

American culture was so strange to me and yet so clearly drawn. There was no ambiguity about Halloween and Thanksgiving or the portraits of Washington and Lincoln. Everyone seemed to know what they meant, and in the same terms.

That Pakistani winter, I smelled library paste for the first time, tasted my first M&M, and read *Henry Huggins and Ribsy*. Mine was a strong conversion, and slowly I began to feel a little part of the gum-cracking, self-assured youth around me. These things that I found so powerful and strange seemed to them as familiar as breathing.

One day, the teacher pulled down the green roller blinds against the glaring noon sun and set a brown metal projector on a desk in the middle of the room. When she snapped it on, the wall filled with scratchy lines. She kerchunked the switch, and slides flicked past us until she reached the title: "A Day on the Farm."

I'd never seen a show like this: the story of a snow-blond boy in cuffed dungarees and a white T-shirt who lived on some sort of cowboy ranch, told entirely in photographs. The pictures were dazzling Technicolor—achingly blue skies, a bright red hat, a plump ginger heifer with soft wavy fur. Each frozen image had a single subtitled sentence telling the story of the boy and his parents. The images were sharp and detailed like a movie but seemed somehow as though they

Nicky (the dog), the author, Nimu and
Pappa Khan, in Lahore, 1969.
Photo by the author's grandmother, Dr. Kate Selzer

must be real. This was an actual boy with this perfect life, roping and milking with a slim, craggy father and a pretty, aproned mother.

The teacher read each subtitle off as it appeared, then toggled the shutter till a new scene came up. Sitting in the muggy dark, I felt far more immersed in the story than in any book I'd ever read. The images on the screen seemed so specific, every detail in sharp relief and full of meaning.

I felt I had to decode each scene, understand exactly what they all meant so I too could become an American, a blond boy on a palomino. Yet as my eyes darted frantically around the frame, it would be replaced by the next one. The story moved inexorably on until it reached "The End" and the fluorescent lights blinked overhead again and the blinds thwopped back against the window frames.

I have forgotten the words to "Shenandoah" and I don't know if they still make library paste. But the story of that boy on the farm, his silky dog and whittling knife, are still vividly mine all these years later. They were the first true taste of the country I have called home for thirty years. ■

END